Pastoral Letters and Instructions, Sermons, Statements and Circulars of Mgsr. Rene Vilatte

1892-1925

Collected and edited by

Serge A. Theriault, Ph.D., Th.D.

THE APOCRYPHILE PRESS
Berkeley, CA

On the first page: coat of arms of Msgr Vilatte.

The Apocryphile Press
1700 Shattuck Ave. #81
Berkeley, CA 94709
www.apocryphile.org

Pastoral Letter & Instructions, Sermons, Statements and Circulars of Msgr. René Vilatte, 1892 – 1925

Copyright © 2017 Serge A. Thériault, Ph.D., D.Th.

ISBN 978-1-944769-74-1

All rights reserved. No part of this publication may be reproduced, stored in a retrieval system, or transmitted in any form or by any means—electronic, mechanical, photocopy, recording, or any other—except for brief quotations in printed reviews, without the prior permission of the publisher.

Printed in the United States of America

Please join our mailing list at
www.apocryphilepress.com/free
and we'll keep you up-to-date on all our new releases
—and we'll also send you a FREE BOOK.
Visit us today!

TABLE OF CONTENTS

INTRODUCTION 5

I
PASTORAL LETTERS AND INSTRUCTIONS 15

II
SERMONS AND SPEECHES 41

III
STATEMENTS AND CIRCULARS 53

Biblical passages quoted 79

Chronology of the Episcopate, 1892-1925 87

Bibliography 101

Annex: Articles of incorporation of the diocese and of the American Catholic Church written by Msgr. Vilatte 115

Notes 127

Msgr. Vilatte was born in Paris on January 24, 1854, of the marriage of Joseph R. Vilatte, merchant, and Marie-Antoinette Chorin. He worked in Canada as a teacher,[1] and was a disciple of the reformer priest Charles Chiniquy,[2] who initiated the Christian Catholic Church. He shared his vision of a purified church that presents the gospel as did the primitive Church; exercises authority according to the democratic spirit of America and seeks the unity for which Christ has prayed.[3]

He was trained by Rev. Chiniquy at his seminary in Sainte-Anne, Illinois, following theological studies at McGill University in Montreal (1881-1883). He was sent by him to Wisconsin and founded parishes there, as well as in Canada, after his ordination by the Christian Catholic Church of Switzerland in 1885. It is a member church of the Old Catholic Movement.

Three years later, the diocese of the Old Catholics of America was established. It was incorporated in Wisconsin and later in Quebec.[4] Msgr. Vilatte was elected first bishop. He was consecrated in 1892,[5] by an independent Catholic church in Sri Lanka, attached to the Patriarchate of Antioch (Syriac).

From 1894, his episcopate was solicited by other national groups of the United States, Polish especially, which he gathered in the American Catholic Church (ACC).[6] "The churches retained their independence and their own pastoral activities."[7] The support of his episcopate was also requested in France and he went to help organize a French Catholic church called Gallican, made possible by the Law of the Cultuelles of 1905.[8]

Bishop Vilatte was a generous humanist and earned the esteem of the church,[9] despite his detractors, until his death in Versailles (France) on 1 July 1929. He had retired there in 1925.

He has left published apological works that can be read online, such as *Ecclesiastical Relations between the Old Catholics of America and Foreign Churches*[10] and *Encyclical to All Bishops Claiming to Be of the Apostolic Succession*. But he is at his best in his pastoral letters and instructions, as well as in his sermons, statements and circulars which are not known, or only partly.

Many of these writings have been lost, including pastoral letters. Only few have survived: the first one, written in October 1892,[11] another in December 1897,[12] and a third, published January 1, 1910,[13] jointly with the bishops of the Polish and Italian constituencies in the United States: Stefan Kaminski and Paolo Miraglia-Gullotti. The first gives the vision of his episcopate in the service of truth; the other underlines the perseverance which must be maintained for this purpose, given the obstacles to be overcome; and the third exposes the faith and ecclesiastical principles of the ACC.

I have found a greater number of pastoral instructions. This is fortunate because Msgr. Vilatte exposes in them his thoughts on questions of Christian life in general (the person of Christ,[14] little things to do during Lent,[15] the obligation to attend Mass[16]) and on subjects peculiar to our rite such as: the Orthodox Catholic faith[17] revealed once for all,[18] and the Holy Spirit who proceeds from the Father.[19]

Also, I was able to get hold of sermons and speeches that have survived, through newspapers and other publications, including those of the Church. It is the case of: *Fighting evil and establishing righteousness*, to knights and commanders of the Order of the Crown of Thorns,[20] *God is with you* at the Polish church in Detroit,[21] *What mean these stones ?*, at the Polish church in Cleveland,[22] *The Church offers you the original Christianity with freedom dear to the Americans*, at a synod in Cleveland,[23] *God is stronger than humans*, at the Church of the Holy Apostles in Paris,[24] *It needs no prophet…*, at the consecration of Bishop Frederic Lloyd in Chicago,[25] *The church is built on the solid rock: Jesus Christ*, at the Polish church in Central Falls, Rhode Island.[26]

Finally, I gathered statements and circulars that give Msgr. Vilatte's perspectives on the establishment of parishes and missions (in Wisconsin,[27] Connecticut,[28] Canada[29]), on the Roman Church (why we are not members,[30] and rejection of its dominance over other churches[31]), chivalry,[32] Christian unity,[33] colonization[34] and works of mercy,[35] in which he has invested himself as a bishop. We add decrees of 1907, confirming Msgr. J. Ernest Houssaye of France,[36] and of 1921 and 1923, authorizing the consecration of the priests George A. McGuire and William Ernest Robertson as bishops of the African Orthodox Church, as well as his statements of June 1907, defining the faith and order of the Église Française (Gallican)[37] and of January 1925, thanking the Gallican bishops for having granted him the title of "patriarch".[38]

I present the texts in the order indicated above. I include some illustrations or photos, and explanatory notes if necessary. At the end of the book will be found: a list of the Biblical passages quoted by

Msgr. Vilatte, with their abbreviations, [39] a chronology of his episcopate (1892-1925), a bibliography containing the list of his publications, and in an annex, the articles of incorporation which he drafted for the diocese and the ACC.

I end this introduction by giving an overview of the theology expressed in these texts. This will, hopefully, facilitate their reading and appreciation.

Theological framework of these texts

An overview of the theology expressed in these texts was given by Bishop Casimir Durand, our second ordinary. He was trained by Msgr. Vilatte and found his writings inspiring, especially the pastoral instructions, sermons and declarations or statements.[40]

Msgr. Vilatte advocated a modern revival of ancient Catholicism, made under the inspiration of Christ, our only Head. He saw the Church "united as in the time of undivided Christianity in the East and West." [41] He did not want to found a new religion, but aspired to live in the Church of the New Testament and the writings of the first centuries.[42] He considered the dogmas of the doctrinal infallibility and the universal jurisdiction of the Bishop of Rome to be erroneous. He did not accept that the dogmatization of these errors by the Pope and the majority of the members of the Vatican Council (1870) suffices to make them truths of faith.[43] He aimed at a reform of theology, against counterfeiting. He also wanted to reform the ecclesiastical structures and restore Christian unity.

He distinguished dogma from theology. He understood dogma in the sense of Christ's words, recorded in Scripture; and theology, as an interpretation of his teachings (to facilitate their acceptance and application). The distinction between the two appears when one uses the criterion of catholicity of Saint Vincent of Lerins: *"is catholic what has been believed everywhere, always and by all."* Bishop Durand wrote: "The churches can not be mistaken if they have always believed in the doctrine taught by the apostles. As to the theological interpretations of the doctrine, they depend on reason, science, history, and the various knowledge which humanity possesses. Thus, faith and freedom are reconciled: faith that does not depend on the whims of schools but on the historical and objective testimony of the Church, and the freedom of criticism or reason, specific to the religious traditions and interests of each particular church." [44]

Faith is the deposit of all the precepts entrusted by Christ to his disciples. It is a deposit which belongs to no one exclusively, but which each church must preserve without omission or addition.[45] Theology, on the other hand, belongs to reason, to history, to criticism, and obeys rules, as is the case with all sciences. The fruits of faith are not to discover new dogmas, nor to complete the revelation transmitted once for all (Jude 3).[46]

How to be the Church that Christ wants is the issue. He established a hierarchy to help believers achieve this goal, not to dominate over them. If anyone wants to be first, it must be to serve his brothers and sisters (Mk 9:35). The primary responsibilities of pastors are to open the conscience of believers and facilitate their enlightenment (Gal 2:20); to act as if they were other Christ. For Msgr. Vilatte, the mission of the Church is purely religious and spiritual. Christ did not give her worldly or temporal authority. To the apostles and disciples He has chosen, He has left strict rules so they be examples for the flock. The first bishops were stewards, not masters (Mt 23:8). The primitive Church was grouped under one chief and lord: Jesus Christ.

"Gradually," wrote Bishop Durand, "ties of brotherhood and charity have been formed between the various local churches, and synods have appeared even before one speaks of general councils. We see that it is necessary to reduce to its original meaning not only the role of the episcopate, but also those of the synod and the council. We are working to bring back the concepts of pastor, bishop, synod, council, ecclesiastical authority and infallibility to the meaning they have in Scripture and ancient traditions. The Church is of monarchical constitution, but it is because of Christ the King, her only monarch. In practice, it is a mere society that has become, in time, a universal republic. The siege of Rome eventually acquired a certain primacy because the city became the capital of the Roman Empire. But it is a primacy of honor, not of jurisdiction."[47] Christ did not take one of his disciples to be a master over others. When he told Peter to feed his lambs and his flock (1 Pet 5:2), it was to restore him to his episcopal function: a function of which he had shown himself unworthy by denying his Lord. As he repented, he deserved to be reinstalled and he was. But it is a mistake to transform this reinstallment into an exaltation above others."[48] Such is the spirit in which Archbishop Vilatte wished to restore the conception of the Church and thus bring a necessary ecclesiastical reform "in capite et in membris".[49]

From the beginning of his ministry, Msgr. Vilatte worked to restore Christian unity. We know his efforts, with Father Chiniquy, "to embrace all Christians, according to the law of the gospel. He encouraged a return to the spiritual union of the origins of the Church: the bond of peace (Eph 4:3) capable of producing the true Christian fraternity in the world. He distinguished essential aspects on which churches must build their unity, such as "the same faith professed in the East and in the West",[50] and secondary ones, such as preserving the autonomy and distinctiveness of each. When all will love each other, and work together for social welfare, spiritually united to Christ, under the constraint of love (Lk 14:23), God reigning in the consciences, then union will be achieved on the contentious points.[51]

In summary, Msgr. Vilatte sees the Church rebuilding its unity under the power of divine Love. This vision is realized with respect for conscience, building the Church on Christ and the truth given once for all to the saints. Professing in the East and the West the faith of the Church which He founded and which the apostles foretold; "not by introducing a vortex of innovations as the West did, while the East held to the Catholicism of the undivided Church."[52]

I
PASTORAL LETTERS AND INSTRUCTIONS

1
DEFENDING ORTHODOX CATHOLIC TRUTH

Pastoral letter of Octobre 1892

In the name of the Trinity One, Most Holy and Adorable, Joseph Rene, by the grace of God the Father, the will of his Son and the inspiration of the Holy Spirit, Metropolitan of the Old Catholics of America, to those that this may concern, health, peace and blessing in the eternal God.

When the Lord, in his plan, dared to elevate us to episcopal dignity, a deep feeling entered our soul, considering our weakness, for faced with difficult circumstances, we understood that we had to rely on the power from on high to be the guardian of the Catholic faith. In spite of our weakness in fulfilling such a noble mission, we have accepted this responsibility, since such was the purpose of God, a desire manifested in an undisputed way for three years.[53]

Today, as in the days of the Apostles, God wanted to choose the least wise among men to confuse the wisest; the poorest to confound the richest, and the weakest to destroy the strongest (1 Cor 1:27-29). So it was neither the wisdom, the nobility of character, nor the wealth that made your pastor the guardian of the One, Holy, Catholic and Apostolic religion.

Yes, God manifested Himself to our unworthiness and commanded us to bear, as a good soldier of Christ, the persecutions of the infidels. It was also from Him that we were commanded to preach to the Gentiles, who then despised our faith, that He might grant them repentance, and bring them back to the right path.

In the presence of the numerous divisions which afflict Christianity, and which are the true consequence of the Roman schism, since the separation of 1054,[54] we must prudently guard against all deceitful appearances, and not depart from the faith of our fathers.

The so-called reform of the 16th century gave birth to so many and so varied hostile sects that the latter led to a real religious Babel, the result of which was the destruction of morality among the people. On all sides we see confusion of tongues, labyrinths of opinions, each trying to emerge from the darkness to arrive at the light that God alone created. Such is the common mistake of Romanism[55] and Protestantism.

In the Christian faith, nothing new can be created, nothing invented or imagined. The true religion of Christ came forth perfect from God and no one may lawfully either add or take away one iota from it. There is no other sure way for those who wander to adventure, at the mercy of error, than to return to orthodox old Catholicism, that is to say, the time when the Church of the East was not less orthodox than the primitive Church of Jérusalem.

Also to submit to the canons, to the dogmas of the Holy Spirit, who spoke to our fathers in different languages and today, speaks to us by the Holy Bible, by the true tradition, in harmony with the eternal Word, and by the seven ecumenical councils inspired by God, who affirmed once and for all the faith delivered to the Saints (Jude 3). The truths, which the ecumenical councils have formulated, are those to which one must believe to be saved. It is the religion preached by the Apostles, against whom "the gates of hell shall not prevail" (Mt 16:18).

O you, beloved of God, remain faithful to that divine faith which will save you, the only one in the world that has the right to be called Orthodox Catholic; do not bring scandal to any of those who are in error. Let us remember that we have a holy mission, whether in the ranks of the clergy or in the circle of the family. Let us always remain worthy of Him who, by special grace, has led us to the only ark of salvation.

Let me also remind you that it is necessary, in the measure of your means, to help Jesus Christ in his poor, to assist the widows and orphans, the sick, the afflicted and our dead. Do not forget, as good and loyal citizens, to pray for your beloved country and for those who govern you, so that peace and prosperity can prevail.

What the world can say about us is of little importance to us so long as our conscience is pure before God, and such being the case, we are entitled to general esteem in all things. In joy as well as in sorrow, we have only to please God and do His will.

We are but a small flock professing the true Catholic faith in this vast new world, and this is the reproach of our adversaries. But the great number of our separated brothers, who live in uncertainty and continual agitation, does not prove that the small number is less fortunate. The Apostles were only twelve, but as we know, a lot came out of this little nucleus.

Honor and glory to God until the end of time. Amen.

Church of St. Marie in Duval, Wisconsin.
This is were was Msgr. Vilatte's cathedra in 1892.

2
ON THE PERSONNE OF OUR LORD JESUS CHRIST

Pastoral Instruction, Advent 1893 [56]

One of the Three Persons, the Word of the Father, descended from heaven of His own Will and of the Will of His Father, and that of the Holy Ghost, and was conceived in the womb of the Blessed Virgin Mary, the Mother of God, by the annunciation of Archangel Gabriel.

He took flesh by the Holy Ghost and of the Blessed Virgin Mary. Divinity united with humanity, and at the end of nine months He was born of her in mystery incomprehensible to nature and the senses, without breaking the seal of virginity of His Mother either at the time of his incarnation, or at any other time before or after.

When He by whose glory the heavens and the earth are filled, was found laid naked in a manger, heavenly and earthly bodies glorified Him. He was wholly in the bosom of His Father and wholly in the manger without being separated. In His Incarnation His divinity was not mixed with his humanity, nor His humanity with His divinity. The natures were preserved without mixture or confusion: His divinity was not separated from His humanity, nor His humanity from His divinity. The union was substantial and inseparable. And the Word was made Flesh and lived with us, as believed by the One, Holy, Catholic and Apostolic Church.

3

WHAT I MAY DO

Pastoral Poem, Lent 1895

I cannot do great things for Him
Who did so much for me;
But I would like to show my love,
Dear Jesus, unto Thee;
Faithful in very little things,
O Saviour, may I be.

There are small things in daily life
In which I may obey,
And thus may show my love to Thee;
And always, every day,
There are some loving little words
Which I for Thee may say.

There are small crosses I may take,
Small acts of faith,
And deeds of love,
Small sorrows I may share;
And little bits of work for
Thee I may do everywhere.

And so, I ask Thee, give me grace
My little place to fill,
That I may ever walk with Thee,
And ever do Thy will;
And in each duty, great or small,
I may be faithful still.

4
WHAT WAS CATHOLIC ONCE MUST BE FOREVER

Pastoral Instruction, July 1895

Seven time, the whole church was represented in council to uphold the purity of the faith, spread over the world, taught alike in East and West. There was only One Church in the world. It was the time of Undivided Christendom. At that time nobody in search of the true Catholic Church could be perplexed or doubtful. The Church was like a city on the top of a mountain, visible everywhere. You could not mistake her, you had no choice, there was no rival.

This state of things continued till the great schism between East and West... The Catholicity of the East was recognized by the West before the latter separated. But the East did not change since, consequently, its Catholicity is unassailable, as it represents the faith of Undivided Christendom, to which every Christian is bound to return, if he does not already belong to it... What was Catholic once must be forever. This is our standoint, our platform. Our orthodox old Catholic church is the true Church instituted by Christ in the West.

There is only One Church which teaches all things whatsoever Christ has commanded and to this church He commands us to convert mankind: "Go ye therefore, and teach all nations," (Mt 28:19-20) and His command is of the most pressing nature, as He Himself shows in the parable of the great supper. The master not only invites his friends and acquaintances, but sends his servant "into the highways and hedges" and tells him to "compel them to come in" (Luke 14:23). Apparently He means to continue its endeavors to bring safely home the poor wanderer lost in the wilderness of unbelief, doubt, heresy and schism. The true shepherd "goeth into the mountains, and seeketh the sheep which is gone astray" (Mt 18:12). He does not stand with folded arms, unconcerned about its fate, coolly waiting for its return, and ready not to shut the gate in its face. The true shepherd in search of the lost sheep does not ask whether he would perhaps "wound the sensibilities" of the stray sheep, it is enough that he knows that the sheep is not on the right way, and consequently he thinks it his duty to call back the poor wanderer, however unwilling the latter may be.

Jesus Christ, our true Shepherd, went on preaching in spite of all resistance, persecution and scorn till they nailed Him to the cross... He will protect His church and ward off the dangers threatening her within and without... The gates of hell shall not prevail against her (Mt 16:18). Arianism,[57] which has already been one of the dominant powers of this world, is gone! Nestorianism,[58] which extended as far as Persia, India, and China, has disappeared! Monophysism,[59] which has already shown vitality and zeal, has disappeared! Romanism, which has already held the West for its own, is now fragmented into a large number of Protestant sects.

While this is our belief, we desire to force no man's assent. Let every human being follow the light of his own conscience. For it is our absolute conviction it is only by so doing he can please the Great Giver of reason. We want freedom to worship God, but we demand equal freedom for our fellow men to worship or abstain from worship, to believe or to disbelieve. In other words, not mere tolerance but perfect liberty for one and all – the believer, the unbeliever, the Catholic, the agnostic, Jew, Turk and Hindu, Parsee and Buddhist.

We are persuaded that if not in this life, then in a life to come, at some time, the TRUTH shall be so presented to the intellect that every rational soul "shall receive the truth, and the truth shall set him free" (John 8:32).

5
THE HOLY GHOST WHO PROCEEDS FROM THE FATHER
Pastoral Instruction, December 1895

The Holy Ghost, proceeding from the Father *and the Son* (Filioque in Latin), is of one substance, majesty, and glory, with the Father and the Son, very and eternal God. I have initialicised the words "and the Son". For it is an indisputable fact, that the addition of these three little words, render the otherwise Orthodox Article, both heterodox and heretical in the opinion of the Greek, Armenian, Syrian, Coptic and Nestorian churches.

All the Eastern churches unanimously teach that the Holy Ghost proceeds from the Father *alone*. The "all" who "acknowledge the perfect orthodoxy" of (the modified) Article is reduced to the Romanists who invented the doctrine of the *Filioque* and made it a dogma, and most of the Reformed churches.

It must be admitted, however, that there is a devout and learned minority at present in the Anglican Communion who repudiate the doctrine that the Holy Ghost proceeded from all eternity out of the Son, and who understand the words "proceeding from the Father and the Son", as referring to the temporal mission of the spirit from the Father and the Son… This Orthodox inclined party would no doubt subscribe to the following statement of faith in the Trinity: "The Father is made of none: neither created nor begotten. The Son is of the Father alone, neither made, nor created *but begotten*. The Holy

Ghost is of the Father alone, neither made, nor created, not begotten, *but proceeding...* " (Jn 15:26)

Assuredly if the *Filioque* is an important truth in itself, and *de fide* in the same sense in which the consubstantiatiality of the Son was *de fide* before the Council of Nicea, then it must be accepted because it would be a part of the original deposit of faith which every Catholic is bound to received.

But the proof that it is no part of the original deposit is that it is neither revealed in Scripture, formulated in symbol by any of the seven Ecumenical councils, nor admitted by the Oriental churches, especially by the Eastern Orthodox Church with whom, like God himself, there is no variableness nor shadow of turning.

The position of the Orientals is that the *Filioque* has not only been irregularly added to the Creed, but that it is false, and makes against the single origin; and therefore against the unity of the Godhead. It is admitted by Latins and Orientals that in the Trinity, Father, Son and Holy Ghost are one in essence, but distinct as persons. Consequently their attributes are of two kinds, essential attributes, common to them all; and distinct personal attributes belonging exclusively to each one of them separately. If we say that procession considered as the eternal act by which the Holy Ghost is produced (and the same for the generation of the Son) is an essential attribute of the Godhead, common to each of the persons, it would follow that the Holy Ghost proceeds not only from the Father and the Son, but also from himself, which is absurd. We can know no more of the mystery of the Trinity than has been recalled by God, and constantly and uniformly taught by the Church.

As to the pretension of those *filioquists* who teach that to deny the procession of the Holy Ghost from the Father is to detract from the dignity and equality of the third person of the Blessed Trinity, we say that it is utterly without foundation. Does it lower the dignity of God the Son, to teach that he is generated by the Father alone? Or is there any more a priori reason why the Holy Ghost should proceed from the Father and the Son, than that the Son should be begotten from all eternity of the Father and the Holy Ghost? No. To the law and the testimonies, and the unvarying voice of the church! The papist argument, to carry their point, is to say that the Son is only a secondary cause or source to the Trinity. But as Guetté[60] well remarks, such an expression cannot be justified by traditional teaching: it is an innovation. Moreover it goes on the supposition that there is something secondary in God. This is contrary to sound Catholic doctrine, and even to simple reason, which shows us that in God there can be nothing but what is necessary.

In conclusion, would it not be advisable, for those who "are waiting and praying for the visible unity of Christendom" to make straight the paths that lead to it? For instance, according to the rule *quod semper...*,[61] would it not be more practical, instead of defending the *Filioque*, to advocate baptism, the confirmation and eucharizing of infants, the doctrine of the transubstantiation[62] of the elements in the Eucharist, unction of the sick, confession as a prerequisite to communion, prayers for the dead...? The septenary number of the sacraments is not found in the Bible nor in the Creeds, but it is unanimously taught by all the Eastern apostolic churches, and is therefor true whether Rome teaches it or not.

So the doctrines and practices above mentioned, they are true because the Orthodox Churches, from the beginning till now, have held and taught them, without reference to the modern Roman church believes or teaches.

Painting of the Holy Trinity that was seen in
Saint Louis Church, Green Bay WI.

6
THINKING OF THOSE WHO SUFFER FOR THEIR FAITH AND NEED TO PERSEVERE IN THE TRUTH

Pastoral letter for the New Year
December 31, 1897

Grace be unto you, and peace from God our Father and from the Lord Jesus Christ (Eph 1:2).

As by the grace of God, we will enter upon a new year in a few hours, it seems good to us to remind you of our brethren in Turkey whom our Holy Patriarch of Antioch is mourning.

May the generosity and Christian nobleness of your hearts bid you to stand before the Throne of God and offer up prayers, alms and sacrifice for those who have shed their blood for Christ's name, and for those who have been left sorrowing.

Let us wish you for this New Year such courage, such devotion and such perseverance for the truth's sake as these poor slain souls possessed. May you all be able to stand firm against the attack of your spiritual ennemies, thanking Almighty God that your religion is not man-made, and remembering that through bearing suffering and sorrow patiently we give glory to God. May your good works be as a *"light that cannot be hid"* (Mt 5:15) to those who are groping in the darkeness which is outside of the One, Holy, Catholic, Apostolic and Orthodox Faith.

And now, imploring God's mercy upon you and wishing you all spiritual and temporal happiness, I remain your affectionate father in God.

Parish church of Green Bay, Wisconsin.
It was from this parish that was issued
the Pastoral Letter for the New Year 1898.

7
WHY IT IS OUR DUTY TO HEAR MASS
Pastoral Instruction, October 1904

Because the Mass is the only service which was instituted by our Lord Jesus Christ, and bequeathed by Him to his Church. (Mt 26:26; Mk 14:22; Lk 22:19)

Because it is that *pure offering*, foretold by Malachi, as a distinguished mark of the Christian Church. (Mal 1:10-11)

Because the doing away of the Daily Service is mentioned in the Holy Scripture as the greatest calamity that can befall the Church. (Dan 8: 11-13)

Because all Christians being an *Holy Priesthood* (1 Pet 11:5-9) are bound to make offerings to God, and we can offer nothing worthy of his acceptance, except "His Beloved Son, in Whom He is well pleased," (Mt 3:17) and Who is present in the Holy Eucharist.

Because the Apostles and Early Christians "continued steadfastly in the Breaking of the Bread and in the accompanying prayers" (Ac 2: 42). These prayers (or Liturgy) are in existence the present day, and many of them are contained in the Missal (or Prayer Book).

Because the Office of the Mass is the oldest form of prayer there is, being compassed, with few exceptions, by the Apostles themselves.

Because we learn from the writings of those who lived in the early age[63] that the Holy Eucharist was always looked upon as The Sacrifice of the Christian Church, and as the Highest Act of Worship that we can pay to God.

Because by this great Act of Worship, the merits of the Sacrifice of Jesus Christ on the Cross are applied to those who worthily assist at it.

Because all those who have sinned owe a sin-offering to God, and there is nothing holy enough to propitiate God, the Father, and to render Him favorable to us except Jesus Christ, the "propitiation for our sins"[64] (1 Jn 2:2) Who is supernaturally present in the Holy Eucharist, and offered to the Father.

Because we owe to God a thank-offering for all his continued mercies to us, and we cannot do this worthily but by offering Him Jesus Christ, "the Lamb without blemishs." (Ex 12:5)

Because, as the creatures of God, we owe Him a continual Sacrifice in acknowledgment of His majesty, and of our absolute dependence on Him; and we can only do this sufficiently by offering Him His Son, co-equal with the Father, "the Mighty God" (Is 9:6) "without Whom was not anything made" (Jn 1:3), and who is called "the Beginning of the Creation of God" (Rev 3:14), and "the first born of every creature" (Col 1:15)

Parishioners coming out of the Mass, Église du Précieux-Sang (Precious Blood Church), Gardner WI, founded by Msgr. Vilatte.

8

OUR FAITH AND ECCLESIASTICAL PRINCIPLES

Pastoral Letter of January 1, 1910

Jointly with Bishops Stefan Kaminski & Paolo Miraglia-Gullotti

In the name of the Father, the Son, and the Holy Spirit, the eternal, consubstantial, and undivided Trinity.

We, by the grace of God and the free suffrages of our faithful, through the Apostolic Succession transmitted lawfully, validly, and canonically to us from the venerable Patriarchal See of the East, founded in Antioch by the blessed Apostle Peter himself which, with the indisputable apostolic authority, rights, and powers, has been continued without interruption unto this day – validly consecrated bishops of the Catholic Church, joined in ecclesiastical union, and canonically assembled in the name of the Lord, in the Orthodox Catholic Cathedral in Buffalo, on this the Feast of the Circumcision of Christ, in the year 1910, do hereby solemnly affirm, repeat, and declare anew, that our Faith and Teaching is the apostolic, orthodox, and catholic doctrine as it has been truly defined, confirmed, and established by the seven ecumenical councils of the undivided Church.

Moreover, in the canonical exercise of our apostolic mission and authority, and especially for the strenghthening of our faithful, and the perfecting of our ministry in the several divisions of the Western Patriarchate, viz., in America, Europe, and Africa, we accept and declare the general authority of the use of the Latin Rite. From the Western Ritual books we are able not only to extract and teach truly and faithfully the apostolic and primitive orthodox doctrine of the Church of Christ, but also, by means of their careful explanation and use, to restore it more and more to its former exalted state.

Furthermore, we exhort with our whole heart and in boundless charity all those who call themselves Christians, who believe and hope in Christ the Incarnate Son of God and Saviour of men, that while preserving and defending all consistent spiritual liberty which is the fruit of righteousness, we may truly become more and more one in faith, hope, and love, offering without ceasing continual prayers and devout petitions to the compassionnate and most high God, beseeching him, the eternal Father of us all, to have mercy on those who are commonly called unbelievers, materialistists, and rationalists, (who through the grievous circumstances of our time are increasing more and more), and to illumine the darkness of their doubting restless minds, so that, converted and led by the Holy Spirit, they may be restored to the communion of the Church of Christ.

Finally, let us both labor for Christian unity, and pray fervently to the Triune God, imploring the hastening of that coming day which is to bring the long-awaited triumph of the one Holy Catholic and Apostolic Church, that glorious future day when all faithful followers of the Incarnate Son of God shall become united again, one fold and one shepherd, who is the risen and ascended Christ alone.

May the Triune God, the Father, the Son, and the Holy Spirit, through the ceaseless proclamation of the Gospel of Christ, favor and assist us in our work for his glory in the Church Militant on eart. Amen.

Msgr. Kaminski, Msgr. Vilatte, Msgr. Miraglia

9

WE MAINTAIN THE FAITH ONCE FOR ALL GIVEN TO THE SAINTS

Pastoral Instruction, 1911

We maintain that the only historical and consistent bond of church unity is that of *"the faith once for all given to the saints"* (Jude 3), as held by the United Church of Christendom, East and West, during the period of the Seven General Councils.

Orthodox Catholics join in faith, hope and love with all churches having the Apostolic ministry and accepting the teaching of the Holy Scriptures as understood by the Fathers, Doctors and Confessors of the undivided Church from which Rome apostatized A.D. 1054.

But valid ministry alone is not sufficient for Christian Catholic unity. Christians must also accept the Apostles and the Nicean Creed without addition or substraction. We likewise acknowledge the dogmatic decrees of the seven Ecumenical Councils as the fundamental basis of unity, and the consentient definitions of the councils of Bethlehem[65] and of Trent[66] concerning the seven sacraments, as being a clear and concise statement of the doctrine held by the Catholic Church throughout the world.

We reject and deny the supremacy or infallibility of any patriarch, or prelate, who demands sole jurisdiction over the Holy Catholic and Apostolic Church of Christ.

We do not adore the images of Jesus Christ, the Blessed Virgin Mary and the Saints but venerate them as sacred things, and representing sacred persons. We believe there is but *"one Mediator of Redemption between God and humanity, Christ Jesus"* (1 Tim 2:5). But that it is a good and useful thing to invoke the Saints who are our glorified brethren, even as we invoke the prayers of our brethren on earth. We allow no dissent in matters of faith for no one has a right to add to or take away from the faith of the Catholic Church.

The day is at end to meet the Lord, and the Spirit of God impels us to cry, *"Maranatha! Come Lord Jesus, come King of Kings"* (Rev 22: 20), for the prosperity of the Christian Church and for its union, let us pray constantly.

II
SERMONS AND SPEECHES

1
FIGHTING EVIL AND ESTABLISHING RIGHTEOUSNESS

To the commanders and knights of the
Order of the Crown of Thorn (OCT)
August 11, 1893

Our Sovereign Lord Jesus Christ teaches us to love God and our fellow beings with all our might, and to believe all which is proposed to us in the Holy Scriptures, by the Church. On the other hand, the arch-enemy, knowing that safety and salvation are only to be found in clinging to the deific faith in Him who was crowned with thorns and crucified, puts forth every effort to estrange us from this belief.

Our vocation as simple Christians places us in the ranks of soldiers of the heavenly King, but our vocation as missioners of philanthropy and whatsoever else is of good report, and our special obligations as warriors of the Holy Temple and of the Crown of Thorns force us still more to cling firmly together, one in heart and purpose, one in obedience to the supreme Grand Master and Chief, to form under His banner a serried and compact army going on conquering and to conquer under the invicible *Sign*. Thus united under the *All Seeing Eye*, arrayed in the armour of brotherly love, armed with good works and knightly deeds, the members of our Order shall go on valiantly against injustice, wrongdoing and impiety. We recognize in the blessed institutions of the OCT a power for fighting evil and the establishing of righteousness.

Let us cherish our beloved Order and though our march be an uphill one and the obstacles to surmount many, still let us take heart, and try to enroll many worthy brethren, that they with us may reap the sure reward. The good works and almsdeeds of the Knights and Ladies will call down upon the Order the benediction of the Grand Architect of the Universe and the gratitude of men.

2

GOD IS WITH YOU

Sermon at the Polish Church in Detroit MI, December 24, 1893

Dear Polish people, you are well known to me. I know your religious zeal, your fidelity, your steadfastness, your self-sacrificing devotion, all your Christian virtues which you show in the service of God, and your faithful steadfast devotion to your Pastor.

Today is the first time we see each other face to face, and so it is only right that I tell you who and what I am. I am a bishop, a Frenchman by birth, a naturalized American and, from the bottom of my heart, a friend of the oppressed, and the sworn enemy of every form of oppression. And that is exactly why I am your friend and well-wisher. On May 29, 1892, I was consecrated for America in Ceylon, in the cathedral there, by the Portuguese Archbishop Alvares, with two Syrian bishops as co-consecrators, namely the Most Rev. Bishops Mar Gregorius of Niranam, and Mar Athanasius of Kottayam. Thousands of Christians turned out for the celebration, and among them was also the United States Consul. He certified the consecration document with his signature and the official seal of our glorious Republic.[67]

I praise God, my dear friends, for the significant and momentuous words by which I was consecrated, and which gave me the authorization to come to you to dedicate your splendid church, making it a House of God, and to lead you on the way to our heavenly homeland. I praise God that those words "Receive the Holy Spirit" were spoken over me by a Latin Archbishop and two Syrian bishops. We have every reason to rejoice over that Syrian episcopal succession which connects us directly with the See of St. Peter, who was the first Bishop of Antioch. Those two pious bishops, upon the express bidding of the present successor of the holy Apostle Peter, the Patriarch of Antioch, took part in my episcopal consecration, and imposed hands on my head. These two bishops, to this very day, use the same language that the Lord of the Church, our loving Savior, used in speaking with his disciples, and which the Blessed Virgin Mary and St. Joseph used while on this earth.

I declare all the sacraments conferred by your parish priest, Fr. Kolasinski, valid and good. He has, with the help of God, brought together this great congregation. God is with the Polish people of Fr. Kolasinski's church.

Interior view of Detroit church, dedicated by Msgr. Vilatte

3
WHAT MEAN THESE STONES?

At the dedication of a new Polish church in Cleveland, Ohio[68]

August 19, 1894

My dearly beloved Polish people, we are here today, by divine permission, to dedicate this home of worship of our Lord Jesus Christ. But the people of Cleveland have a right to ask of us, in the words of the Scriptures, *"What mean ye by these stones?"* (Jos 4:6) The answer we give readily. This church is for the worship of God by his children. It is for the promulgation of the Catholic religion, for we are nothing less that Catholics and remain so, leaving our Catholicism a precious heritage for our children.

Yes, yes, we are Catholics. Let us ever remain so, never relinquishing an iota of our Catholic dogma even though we do insist on our right to hold property in our own names. These stones have their meaning. They signify that this is a church in which the true Catholic religion is to be taught and the true God is to be worshiped.

My dear Polish people, I am an American Catholic bishop and you are an American Catholic people. This land of liberty we love and will defend, giving, if need be, our lives for its sake. Let these stones mean this also to the people of Cleveland.

Let us be ever faithful to the Catholic religion, pure and undefiled, being guilty of neither adding to its dogma nor subtracting therefrom as many who have expounded its faith have done in the past. Let us also be patriotic and true to our dear country. Let us further not be forgetful of the interests and needs of your beloved Poland.

4
THE CHURCH OFFERS YOU PRIMITIVE CHRISTIANITY, AND WITH IT LIBERTY

At the founding Synod of the American Catholic Church (ACC) in Cleveland, August 20, 1894

We are met together to exclaim: *"Magna est Veritas et praevalebit / Great is the truth and it shall prevail!"* (Esd 4:41) We are met to proclaim all over the land: "Beware of despotism if you love liberty."

In rejecting false doctrines, we have put ourselves in doctrinal harmony with the East, and entered into unity of spirit with the Ecumenical Thrones of Jerusalem, the mother of all the churches, and Antioch, Constantinople, Alexandria, and the "Old Catholics" of Holland, Germany, France, Switzerland, and Ceylon. We recognize the Ecumenical Concils as the fountain head for the unity of faith. Keep intact this sacred deposit of the faith. The ACC offers you primitive Christianity, and with it what all Americans dearly cherish: liberty.

The ACC will be composed of the different nationalities of the old world, yet here united to one great American nation, and led by chief pastors who, being Catholic in faith and thoroughly American in spirit, are yet adapted to understand and enter into several national peculiarities of their respective flocks.

The new Church will favor the education of children of the congregations in the public schools of America. It is also in favor of the utmost freedom of discussion of all subjects pertaining to religion.

Polish Church (ACC), Cleveland, 1894

5

**WITHSTAND OPPOSITION:
GOD IS STRONGER THAN HUMANS**

Excerpts from speeches made in France

A

At the first Mass of the parish of the Holy Apostles,
22 Legendre Street in Paris, February 3, 1907

I have been working for several years as a missionary. I traveled through America and India, and no one stopped me from speaking. We will not let ourselves be influenced: God is stronger than humans.

The parish has the right to exist. It is legally constituted by virtue of the Law of the Cultuelles of 1905. The Roman rite is a fraction, not the whole, of universal Catholicism.

But even to those who interrupt and insult me, I say that I will not excommunicate them. I wish you no harm. God be with you.

B

Celebrating parish confirmations at Contréglise (Haute Saône)
on 23 May 1907

Dear parishioners, present a united front in the face of opposition and support your parish priest. France and the whole of Europe have their eyes turned towards Contréglise

6
IT NEEDS NO PROPHET...

Excerpt from the sermon preached at the consecration of
Msgr. Frederic Lloyd as Bishop of Illinois, on December 19, 1915

It needs no prophet to foretell for you and the American Catholic Church a great future in the Province of God. The need fo a Church both American and Catholic, and free from paparchy and all foreign powers, has been felt for many years by Christians of all the denominations. May your zeal and apostolic ministry be crowned with success.

Msgr. Vilatte and Msgr. Lloyd,

with priests Francis Kanski and Timothy Peshkoff

7
THIS CHURCH IS BUILT ON CHRIST, THE ROCK THAT NEVER FAILS.

Sermon preached at the laying of the foundation stone of a Polish church in Central Falls, R.I., on May 18, 1919.

I felicitate you for your wonderful accomplishment and I trust that you will all remain faithful to the Church.

This church is built on Jesus Christ; it is built on the rock that never fails (1Tim 1:1; Rom 5:5). Put your trust in Him, be honest, good, frank Christian Catholics.

Preach the doctrine of peace, not of war.[69] We have had war and it is over. Now go forth and preach the doctrine of peace, the Word of God.

I urge you to send your children to school and to see to it that they are taught to read and write, and to speak the English language. Teach your children to know this great, glorious country of America that they may become worthy citizen.

And may the blessing of God Almighty: the Father, the Son, and the Holy Spirit, be with you and abide in you. Amen.

III
STATEMENTS AND CIRCULARS

1
ESTABLISHMENT OF PARISHES AND MISSIONS

A
Walhain, Wisconsin, May 14, 1891[70]

Three years ago several families from Walhain came to Dyckesville asking that I open an Old Catholic Mission among them. During these three years the desire has become stronger and stronger, and it was arranged that Ascension Day 1891 should be solemnly observed, and that thereafter the mission should be regularly visited by a priest every other Sunday. The families interested furnished a suitable hall for temporary use. A piece of land has also been donated by one family as a site for a new church (dedicated to Saint Joseph), clergy house and cemetery... The site is beautifully situated on an eminence overlooking the country around about for many miles in each direction...

Walhain parish church, at the corner of
State Highway 54 & Walhain Road

B
Green Bay, Wisconsin, August 25, 1892

To the reporter who asks me why we come to celebrate in Green Bay, I say: 17 years ago, Roman Catholics in this city had a church that is not used, and as we receive requests from people who want religious services, my duty is clear and I have decided to offer them to those who accept our doctrine.

Do not misunderstand me: I am not opposed to any religious denomination whatsoever. But since no religious service is offered in this neighborhood, and the good people of this locality have asked me to come, I have acted on their request. Services will be provided regularly on the east side of the river in the building we are using on a temporary basis. In due course, a beautiful church will be built.

C
Danielson, Connecticut, February 17, 1896

French Canadians predominated in Saint James Parish[71] and you were right to start your claim in 1894: the bishop should not have refused you to have your separate parish. I am willing to help you organize your national parish[72] under our aegis.[73]

D
Saint Joseph Island (Ontario), Canada, January 1902

Msgr. Vilatte founded a mission among the French Canadians and the Chippewa Indians of Saint Joseph Island.[74] He was very active on the island, saying mass regularly in the chapel of the mission and traveling through the woods, even to the neighboring islets.

"Christmas was celebrated with great pomp, can we read in <u>The St Joe Herald</u>. I said the midnight Mass, assisted by three other officiating ministers.[75] The sermon was said in English and in French. The chapel was too small to receive all the faithful who came from all parts of the island. The altar and the chapel were flooded by light, splendidly decorated with flowers and greenery. This service was the most beautiful that was ever held on the Island and it will never be forgotten by those who attended. In the afternoon we had Vespers, followed by several baptisms.

We have just acquired a piece of land, where we will establish a cemetery. It is touching to see the army of workers who came to clear it and fence it. The cemetery was unfortunately necessary, for we have just lost a very devoted sister. I will dedicate it in the spring, as well as the mortuary chapel."

Chapel of St Joseph Island Mission
at Gawas Bay

2

WHY WE ARE NOT ROMANIST

Statement of December 1895

All the Roman Church hold in common with the Catholic churches we accept; but what she holds over and above we reject. That is, we do not accept her peculiarities which are Roman but not Catholic.

We are not Romanists because we cannot accept the Papal theory of church government,viz that all church authority is derived from the See of Rome, and that no Bishop can have mission otherwise than through the See of Rome.

In the Acts of the Apostles where we find the account of the formation of the first Christian churches, we do not find the faintest trace of the supremacy or omnipotence of the Bishop of Rome or of St. Peter. The Apostles formed churches by preaching the gospel and ministering the sacraments of the church. Thus people were called out and incorporated into independent or national churches. St. Paul left behind him officers of the church, charged with the powers of transmitting the Episcopal authority on to others. But there is no allusion to St. Paul or others receiving their commission from St. Peter, but from the Lord Jesus Christ immediately.

The doctrine of Supremacy and Infallibility are peculiar to the Roman Church. They are based upon the assumption that Peter was the only Vicar of Jesus Christ and the only head of the church. In the New Testament there is not the faintest whisper that St. Peter was ever in Rome at all and that he was martyred there.[76] The fabric of the Papacy therefore rests upon scarcely any foundation whatever.

"Babylon" in St.Peter's first epistle (1 Pet 5:13) is made to signify "Rome," a very shaky ground to rest upon! [77]

Surely, if the theory of the Papal supremacy were correct, we should find some mention of it in the Acts of the Apostles and Our Lord would have given us at least some foundation. The doctrine that St. Peter was the only head of the church was never systematized till of late years, when it was put forth by the Jesuit Salmeron.[78]

The Roman church says: "The Bishop of Rome was always looked upon as Chief authority in the church: his was always the primatial See, and he was universally acknowledged as the first Bishop of Christendom." Rome being the metropolis of the Western Empire, its Bishops's supremacy was a political supremacy, a matter of ecclesiastical convenience, due to his being the Bishop of the capital city of the Roman Empire. The supremacy was never given to him by God.

We cannot be Roman Catholics because we consider it altogether wrong to *de-catholicise* the great Eastern churches, which are Catholic just as much, to say the least, as the Roman church or ourselves. All those who held the Catholic doctrines and creeds, who have apostolic succession and orders, and the same divine service and worship are Catholics. The Roman church tries to *de-catholicise* them because they do not hold the Papal supremacy and do not acknowledge the jurisdiction of the See of Rome.

Finally, we are not Romanists because we wish to remain faithful to the true Catholic Faith as set forth by the General Councils of the Undivided Church, and decline to accept any doctrinal novelties invented by the Bishop of Rome. [79]

3
WORKING FOR THE GREAT END OF UNITY

Statement of July 1895

It is not only by prayer, all important as that is, that the faithful are called to work for the great end of Unity. Religious differences tend towards a certain uncharitableness of thought and of speech, which in their turn increase these differences and become the greatest obstacles to reunion.

Let us therefore, in addition to our prayers, keep a strict guard over our toughts and words; let us be just and generous in our judgements and criticisms of those who are separated from us, and so help in a most practical way to remove the obstacles which hinder the fulfilment of our Master's will (Jn 17:21); yet let us pray to the Lord for the peace of the whole world, the good estate of the holy churches of God and the union of them all.

"Blessed are you when people hate you and when they exclude you and revile you and spurn your name as evil, on account of the Son of Man! Rejoice ye in that day, and leap for joy: for, behold, your reward is great in heaven: for in the like manner did their fathers unto the prophets." (Lk 6:22-23)

4
PROMOTING IMMIGRATION IN CANADA AS COLONIZING BISHOP

Project presented to Mr. James Smart,
Deputy minister of Interior in Ottawa, April 1, 1902

I would like to form a colony in Western Canada, which would be made of farmers of my faith and others from Europe: Swiss, French and Belgians.

I need your help to locate a land, obtaining back up, protection and pamphlets about agricultural lands in Canada, free traveling fare on railway, as well as authority and power to go speak and give lectures about the fertility and glory of Canada to farmers in Europe.

I must take possession of the land and build at once my residence and an Immigration House in the middle of the new colony so to be the pioneer, the heart and the soul of the place, and in good time welcome the new settlers.[80]

Allocated land was near Rosthern, Saskatchewan

5

THE ORDER OF THE CROWN OF THORNS, APOSTOLIC AND PHILANTHROPIC

A circular of 1904

The aims of the Knightly and Religious Order of the Crown of Thorns are: to defend the divinity of Jesus Christ, to adore Him and to honor the suffering which He endured in the Passion, particularly from the Holy Crown of Thorns; to reward those who have distinguished themselves in the interest of Jesus Christ, of Humanity, of the Order and of its Apostolic and Philanthropic work; and to recompense those who relieve the poor in distress, to help the widow and fatherless, and to encourage virtue, frugality, arts, industry and patriotism.

Ladies are admitted into the Order with the title of *Lady of Honor and Devotion of the Crown of Thorns.*

The jewel of the Order is a Cross of Jerusalem in white enamel, surrounded by a Crown of Thorns in gold. In the center of the Cross is a shield with the monogram Chi Rho in gold, and carries with it the title of *Doctor Christianissimus (D.Chr.).*

Saint Louis holding the Crown of Thorns
Painting by Le Sueur, 17th century

6

ROME ARROGATES ITSELF A POWER OF DISCIPLINE OVER THE OTHER CHURCHES THAT I NEITHER ADMIT NOR RECOGNIZE

Declaration of March 14, 1907, commenting on his excommunication of June 13, 1900, by the Roman authorities, for having consecrated Rev. Paulo Miraglia-Gullotti as bishop.

That act of exclusion does not touch me, given that neither as a priest, nor as a bishop, have I been part of the Roman Communion.

The Church of Rome arrogates itself a power of universal discipline over the other Churches, even those separate from her. I neither admit nor recognize that power.

I know that Christ died to save all those who believe in Him, and not only those who believe in the Pope, Bishop of Rome. Neither my conscience nor my will is in any way troubled by anathemas launched by a human power that numerous Churches, forming the majority of Catholic Christendom, refuse to acknowledge as having an exclusive domination.

I pray Christ, sole head of the great Church, to pardon those who abuse His name, to detach them from a sectarian spirit and unite them at last to the universal communion.

7
CONFIRMATION OF MSGR. JULIEN HOUSSAYE AS METROPOLITAN OF FRANCE

May 7, 1907

We hereby renew
and confirm our brother
Julien Houssaye,
consecrated by Bishop Paul Miraglia
on 4 December 1904,
in Thiengen (Germany),
in his dignity of
Metropolitan Archbishop of France.

Consequently, the bishops consecrated by us,
as well as the priests, must be in union with him
as he is in union of faith with us.

Msgr. Houssaye and Msgr. Miraglia

Statement of Faith and Order

Formulated jointly with the bishop and clergy in France
June 1907

Faith

- One Chief, Jesus Christ, the same for all true Christian churches.

- One infallibility, that of the Holy Scriptures, inspired by God and accepted by all Christian communions.

- Everything the Universal Church has taught before Roman Church pretentions caused the great schism of the East (1054).

- All the creeds and doctrines of the Ecumenical Councils till the 7th century.

- Seven sacraments: Baptism, Confirmation, Eucharist, Penance, Marriage, Holy Orders, Anointing of the Sick.

- Blessed Virgin Mary and Saints honored, not as divine beings but as human creatures having the dignity to be models for humankind.

- Holy Mysteries and other church services, sermons by the clergy, books of Old and New Testament distributed to be read and meditated by the faithful, and family prayers in homes.

Order

- Bishops, priests and deacons elected according to Apostolic practice so that they be servants and not masters of the faithful.

- A National Church linked to other Christian churches by the common faith in Jesus Christ but independent in its organization.

- Bishops chosen among the more meritorious priests, having no fastuous court, nor temporal and jurisdictional privileges but the spiritual powers of superintendants.

- Episcopal authority not centralized in the hands of one of them.

- The general and supreme government of the church belongs to the general assembly of the clergy and the faithful gathered in synods.

- All those who believe in Christ and in the divine inspiration of the bible are recognized and saluted as brothers (and sisters) whatever be the doctrinal interpretation made in each particular church. We do not allow our diversity to divide us. Instead, we long with charity for what unites us in the faith.

- There is no change as to rites and usages which are those of the Latin Church unless the general assembly decides otherwise (to make the church more conform to Apostolic traditions).

9
TAKING CARE OF PEOPLE IN NEED AND OFFERING A HEALTHY AND AUTONOMOUS LIFE

Excerts from the circular *Vilatteville, Chihuahua, Mexico: a farming community under the aegis of the Society of the Precious Blood*
July 18, 1910

The *Society of the Precious Blood*, under Archbishop Vilatte, is an institution established for the glory of God, the sanctification and education of its members, and the propagation of charitable and philanthrophic work, for the benefit of all.

Come unto me all of you who are suffering and I will resfresh you (Mt 11:28). These are the words of Jesus Christ; this is also our password: If God sees it fit to bless our hard and harduous work of tilling the soil in Vilatteville, our harvest will care for the orphans and the cripples, for the friendless or senior citizen, who have no other abode in which to spend the few remaining years of their life, and educate a new generation for the struggle of the world.

But our work will not stop there. The land of Vilatteville must be the partage of the people of good will and good fellowship. Be your own master, have your own home, take for your children and you a piece of the earth, and bring up your family under the shadow of our institution.

All the year round, Mother Earth in Vilattleville will provide for your store, she is too good to strike... This is the land to which we are going, the land of health, peace and rest...

Love for all humanity, charity, philanthropy and success for you and your little one, far from the furnace of speculation, despotism and deception.

Knock at the door and we will give hospitality during those few days that you will need to select your land and start the foundation of your home.

And in the years to come, if your recognize the good that we have done to you and those you love, bless our memory for ever.

10
WE SHOULD BE READY TO AID ALL WHO COME TO US, OR WHOM WE MAY DISCOVER IN DISTRESS

Excerpts from the circular Orphan and Convalescent Home of St. Mary of Nazareth, Autumn 1919

St. Mary's Home's object is to feed the hungry, clothe the naked, to receive orphans between the ages of 5 and 16 years, without distinction of creed or nationality... St. Mary's is also designed to care for those who, after being discharged from the hospital, still find themselves too weak to resume their daily work.

We are espacially involved in the welfare of Syrian, Armenian, Greek, Oriental, and other foreign orphans, whom it is our desire to serve. We labor to have such children educated in the public schools and to become patriotic Americans. We consider it our duty to do all in our power to make such orphans true Americans, loyal to the flag, and emancipated from all foreign control.

Jesus declared: "If anyone gives even a cup of cold water to one of these little ones who is my disciple, truly I tell you, that person will certainly not lose their" (Mat 10:42). We should make our charity reach out to the needy humanity and be ready to aid, to the best of our ability, all who come to us, or all whom we may discover in distress. Jew or Christian, Bouddhist or Mohammetan, we are all children of our heavenly Father, and the divine commandment is: « Let us love one another, for love comes from God. Everyone who loves has been born of God and knows God » (1 Jn 4:7).

We are convinced that a kind heart, a sympathetic word to a person in dire distress will please God more than all the gorgeous rituals of all the churches where love of mankind is absent: "Suppose a brother or a sister is without clothes and daily food.[16] If one of you says to them, "Go in peace; keep warm and well fed," but does nothing about their physical needs, what good is it?" (1 Jas 2:15-16) Rather let us fulfill the royal law: "Thou shall love thy neighbor as thyself" (Mt 22: 39). Our mission is founded on this precept, following in the footstep of Him who "went alout doing great" and who said: "Truly I tell you, whatever you did for one of the least of these brothers and sisters of mine, you did for me." (Mat 25:39-40)

11
DECREES ALLOWING CONSECRATION AND GRANTING COMMISSION TO ASSIST IN LAYING-ON OF HANDS

1921

We grant unto the Right Rev. Carl A. Nybladh of the Swedish American constituency, commission to assist us in the laying-on of hands and consecration to the Sacred Order of the Episcopate of the **Reverend George Alexander McGuire**, Priest and Bishop-elect of the African Orthodox Church, which will be celebrated and performed on Wednesday the 28th day of September 1921 in the Church of Our Lady, 4429 North Mulligan Avenue, Norwood Park, County of Cook, Illinois. Given on September 27, 1921.

1923

We, hereby, allow the consecration of the **Reverend William Ernest Robertson**, Priest ordained by us in 1921. We stand before God's majesty and raising up our hands towards this Venerable Priest pray that the Holy Ghost descend upon him, as He did upon the Apostles and were authorized to bind and loose as written by St. Matthew (Mt 16:19). We, therefore, by virtue of our authority received from God, authorize His Grace, the Most Rev. George Alexander McGuire, to consecrate in episcopal dignity the Priest W.W. Robertson elected Auxiliary Bishop under the jurisdiction of our well-beloved Brother G.A. McGuire. Given on October 10, 1923, in our Chapel Notre Dame of France.

12
MOVED BY THE TITLE OF PATRIARCH

To the Gallican Episcopate
Att: Msgr. Pierre G. Vigué
January 22, 1925

I am deeply moved by the title of "patriarch" which you have granted to me, although I do not consider myself worthy of this honor.

I know enough the generosity of your hearts to pay homage to it, even publicly, and I am sure of your gratitude for what I did for the Gallican Church.

I return your good wishes and ask God, in this age of atheism, to bless your efforts for the greater good of souls who are in search of the truth.

To those who signed the letter addressed to me, receive the assurance of my humble prayers and of my devotion to our Lord and Savior Jesus Christ.

Msgr. Robertson (1st), Msgr. McGuire (2nd) and other bishops of the African Orthodox Church

Gallican Primate L.F. Giraud (2nd), ordained priest by Msgr. Vilatte and consecrated by Msgr. Houssaye, and Msgr. Vigué (1st) consecrated by him.

BIBLICAL PASSAGES QUOTED

Acts of the Apostles (Act) 2:42	They devoted themselves to the apostles' teaching and to fellowship, to the breaking of the bread and to prayer.
Colossians (Col) 1:15	He is the image of the invisible God, the firstborn of all creation.
1 Corinthians (Cor) 1:27-29	God has chosen the foolish things of the world to shame the wise, and God has chosen the weak things of the world to shame the things which are strong.
Daniel (Dan) 8:11-13	The regular sacrifice was removed from him, and the sanctuary was thrown down... Then I heard: "How long will the vision about the regular sacrifice apply, while the transgression causes horror, so as to allow both the holy place and the host to be trampled?"
Ephesians (Eph) 1:2	Grace and peace to you from God our Father and the Lord Jesus Christ.
1 Esdras (Esd) 4:41 [81]	Great is the truth and it will prevail. Often in latin: *Magna est veritas et praevalebit.*
Exodus (Ex) 12:5	It will be a lamb without blemish, a male of the first year.
Isaiah (Is) 9:6	For unto us a Child is born, a Son is given; and the government will be upon His shoulder. And His name will be called Wonderful, Counselor, Mighty God, Everlasting Father, Prince of Peace.

James (Jas) 2: 15-16	If a brother or sister is naked and destitute of daily food, and one of you says to them, "Depart in peace, be warmed and filled," but you do not give them the things which are needed for the body, what does it profit?
John (Jn) 1: 3	All things were made through Him, and without Him nothing was made that was made.
Jn 8: 32	You shall know the truth, and the truth shall make you free.
Jn 15: 26	I shall send to you from the Father, the Spirit of truth who proceeds from the Father.
Jn 17: 21	May they all be one, as You, Father, are in Me, and I in You; may they also be one in Us, that the world may believe that You sent Me.
1 John (Jn) 2: 2	He Himself is the propitiation for our sins, and not for ours only but also for the whole world.
1 Jn 4: 7	Let us love one another, for love is of God; and everyone who loves is born of God and knows God.
Joshua (Jos) 4: 6	May this be a sign among you when your children ask in time to come, saying, "What do these stones mean to you?"

Jude (Jud) 3	The faith was once delivered to the saints.
Luke (Lk) 6:22-23	Blessed are you, when others shall hate you, and when they shall separate you from their company, and shall reproach you, and cast out your name as evil, for the Son of man's sake. Rejoice in that day, and leap for joy: for your reward is great in heaven.
Lk 14:23	The lord said to the servant, Go out into the highways and hedges, and compel them to come in, that my house may be filled.
Lk 22:19	Jesus took bread, and gave thanks, and brake it, and gave unto them, saying, This is my body which is given for you: this do in remembrance of me.
Malachi (Mal) 1:11	In every place incense shall be offered unto my name, and a pure offering: for my name shall be great among the heathen, said the Lord of hosts.
Mark (Mk) 14:22	Jesus took bread, and blessed, and brake it, and gave to them, and said, Take, eat: this is my body.
Matthew (Mt) 3:17	A voice from heaven said, This is my beloved Son, in whom I am well pleased.
Mt 5:15	We don't light a candle, and put it under a bushel, but on a candlestick; and it gives light to all that are in the house.

Mt 10:42	Whosoever shall give to drink to one of these little ones a cup of cold water only in the name of a disciple, shall in no wise lose his reward.
Mt 11:28	Come to me, all you that labour and are heavy laden, and I will give you rest.
Mt 16:18	The gates of hell shall not prevail against my church.
Mt 18:12	If a man have an hundred sheep, and one of them be gone astray, doesn't he leave the ninety-nine, and seek that which is gone astray?
Mt 22:39	You shall love your neighbour as yourself.
Mt 25:39-40	When did we see you sick, or in prison, and came to you? And the King shall answer and say to them, Inasmuch as you have done it to one of the least of these my brethren, you have done it to me.
Mt 26:26	Jesus took bread, and blessed it, and brake it, and gave it to the disciples, and said, Take, eat; this is my body.
1 Peter (Pet) 2:5	As lively stones, you are built up an holy priesthood, to offer up spiritual sacrifices, acceptable to God by Jesus Christ.

1 Pet 5:13	The church that is at Babylon, elected together with you, salutes you.
Revelation (Rev) 3:14	(He is) the Amen, the faithful and true witness, the beginning of the creation of God.
Rev 22:20	*Maranatha!* Come, Lord Jesus!
Romans (Rom) 5:5	Hope does not put us to shame, because God's love has been poured out into our hearts through the Holy Spirit, who has been given to us.
1 Timothy (Tim) 1:1	Paul, an apostle of Christ Jesus by the command of God our Savior and of Christ Jesus our hope.
1 Tim 2:5	There is one mediator between God and humanity, Jesus Christ.

.

CHRONOLOGY OF THE EPISCOPATE
1892-1925

1892: Consecration of Msgr. Vilatte on May 29, by Msgr. Antonio F.X. Alvares, Archbishop of the Western Rite under Antioch (Independent Catholic Church of Ceylon, Goa and India), assisted by the Syriac Antiochean Archbishops of Niranam and of Kottayam, India: Mar George Gregorius (St. Gregory of Parumala[82]) and Mar Paul Athanasius. He inaugurated his episcopal ministry at Duval on August 5. English-speaking mission established in West Sutton, Massachusetts in the month of August. Edward R. Knowles ordained as priest in charge. First Mass of Green Bay Mission on August 24 (25 families). Started publication of a diocesan paper called **The Old Catholic**.

1893: Appointed Grand Master (G.M.) of the Order of the Crown of Thorns (OCT) in succession to G.M. the Rev. Gaston Fercken. Published *Statutes of the OCT (*August 11). Had a booth at the World Parliament of Religions held in Chicago from September 11 to 18. New church (St. Joseph) established at Walhain, Brown County, on All Saints Day. Also in November, published *Encyclical to All the Bishops Claiming to Be of the Apostolic Succession* and the booklet *St. Peter in Rome*? Episcopal ministration to Independent Polish Catholics: dedicated a church for them at Detroit, Michigan, on December 24. Rector Dominic Kolasinski incardinated.

1894: Father Florent de Menlenane, a priest in Roman Orders, received for ministry at Duval and Green Bay. Sisters Marie Ashmun and Anne Schoen joined the Society of the Precious Blood (SPB). Synod of Cleveland, Ohio, held August 19-20: church declared composed of different nationalities. Polish church dedicated and priests ordained (A. Kolaszewski and S.

Kaminski). American Catholic Church (ACC) established as council of churches and Polish-speaking constituency organized.

1895:   Church of St. Louis de France inaugurated in Green Bay. Rev. B.E. Harding appointed rector. Also installed as Grand Prior of the OCT and Superior of the SPB. All Saints Polish Parish, Chicago, and its rector Anton Kozlowski received into the church.

1896:   ***Smaller Missal*** published on January 9. Beginning of Quebec missions on May 5. Reverend Etienne Côté pastor in Montreal, and Reverend J.B. Gauthier, in Sainte Ursule, Maskinonge County. Polish parish established at Buffalo, New York on May 20. In May, Anthony Pilzak ordained for a Lithuanian Mission in Buffalo. The same month, meeting with group of French Canadians from Danielson, Connecticut (M. Bessette, E. Jetté, C. Leclair) who wanted to organize a national parish. Valentine Gawrychowski and Casimir Grzybowski ordained 14 August in Green Bay for Polish ministry. Also ordained: Edward Donkin for St. Louis, Green Bay (October 26), and Édouard Bovard, Nicolas Pleimling and George Reader for ministry in Wisconsin. At a synod held in Buffalo (50 delegates) on September 19, the Rev. S. Kaminski was elected as coadjutor bishop in charge of the Polish constituency.

1897: Project of having SPB religious live under Benedictine Rule approved. Leader: Rev. B.E. Harding, who took the name Brother William. On August 7, 100 acres of land bought in Emery, Wisconsin. Sisters Marie and Anne were part of the project. Their goal was to open an orphanage in the monastery. Episcopal election of Rev. Kaminski confirmed by the church based on the positive results of a consultation launched on May 11 (Rev. E. Donkin in charge). Rev. Kozlowski of Chicago did not acquiesce in the result and was consecrated rival bishop by European Old Catholics at Berne on November 21. St. Mary's Church opened in Buffalo on October 1 by Rev. Donkin. Clergy conference held in Chicago on December 16.

1898: In the month of February, decision made to transfer the episcopal see to Canada. Rectories and lands at Duval and Green Bay were sold. Money to be used to buy land and property in Saint Joseph Island (Algoma County), Ontario (June 8, 1898). On March 21, consecrated Rev. Stefan Kaminski in Buffalo. On April 19, ordained Flavien A. Minguy (born in Quebec City) as parish priest for St. Mary's, Duval. Traveled to the United Kingdom. In June, visited Bishop Frederick G. Lee of the Order of Corporate Reunion, in Dorchester. Stayed with Benedictine Monks at Llanthony Abbey, South Wales. On July 27, ordained priest Dom Ignatius of Jesus (J.L. Lyne) and blessed him as Father Abbot of the monastery. He also ordained Dom Itud Mary of the Epiphany (A.C. Cobb) and blessed Mother Tudfil (Jessie Dew) as Prioress.

1899: In January, spent time with Dom Jean Parisot at the Benedictine Abbey of Ligugé in Poitou, France. Dom Parisot authored the book ***Mgr Vilatte, fondateur de l'Église vieille-catholique en Amérique***. Through his instrumentality, Bishop Vilatte became Grand Master of the Order of the Militia of Jesus Christ. Also, in the same year, he became Grand Master of the Order of the Lion and Black Cross (OLBC).

1900: Franco-American House established at 199 Pereire Blvd in Paris. On May 6, he consecrated Padre Paulo Miraglia-Gullotti as Bishop for an Italian constituency and as Prelate Commander of the OCT. Also, church project in France, with OCT Knight the Rev. J.E. Houssaye. Priests A. Ribourg and J. Constantin ordained in Paris. Death of former diocesan trustee Augustin Marchand on October 8. Burial in Duval by Father F.A. Minguy. Mission Notre Dame du Lac (Our Lady of the Lake) inaugurated in mid-October on Saint Joseph Island (Algoma), Ontario, Canada.

1902: In January, published ***Letter Concerning the Acceptance of the Protestant Episcopal Faith by Bishop Kozlowski***. Also through correspondence with the Department of Interior in Ottawa (1902-1904), he developed a scheme for establishing a community church colony in Western Canada with farmers from Europe. Also helped in the development of the mission in Montreal. Admitted to the

OCT the Rev. Dr. Ernest C. Margrander, professor of theology in Chicago.

1903: On April 3, ordained Franciszek Kanski priest for the Polish Parish of Transfiguration in Chicago. On June 14, he consecrated the Rev. Henry Marsh-Edwards bishop at Bournemouth for the church in England. He also ordained two priests, (possibly) including former Llanthony Abbey monk Maurice G. Stannard.

1904: Made Dr. Margrander his theological advisor. Gave Msgr. Miraglia-Gullotti of Italy authority to consecrate the Rev. J.E. Houssaye bishop for France and Prelate Commander of the OCT, 4 December. Ordained T. Jakimowicz, A. de Lubicz, J. Tomaszewski and Gustave Panchaud for ministry in Greater Chicago.

1905: Law of Separation of Church and State promulgated in France (9 December). Associations for the exercise of Religion (Cultuelles) instituted. Clergy conference held in Chicago on December 17. Priests renewed their vows to Msgr. Vilatte.

1906: In France, helped priests and politicians to structure a Gallican Catholic Cultuelle.

1907: Leader of the Gallican cultuelle centered in Paris. On January 23, inaugurated Église des Saints-Apôtres at 22 Legendre Street. Priests incardinated: P. Fatôme, G. Darragon, F. Meillon, L.A. Duhamel, J. Ruelle. Ordained Louis-François Giraud (June 21), who was to become his

Vicar General in France. Italian-American constituency formed under the Rev. Luigi Lops. Centre in Youngstown OH, dedicated to San Rocco.

1908: Back in North America, Msgr Vilatte stayed in Montreal. Around that time he ordained Ed O'Neill priest for ministry in Canada. Msgr. Miraglia-Gullotti appointed bishop auxiliary, in charge of the Italian-American constituency. Before leaving Europe for the U.S.A., he was granted authority to consecrate William P.
Whitebrook as bishop for the church in England, on December 27. Father William (Harding), SPB, and five religious formed the Benedictine Abbey of St. Dunstan.

1909: Presided over synod at Notre Dame Polish Church in Winnipeg. Received Rev. Paul Markiewicz into the clergy and ordained two monks from Llanthony Abbey (South Wales): Gildas Taylor and Asaph Harris (also blessed as Abbot in succession to Dom Ignatius). In the Spring, took up residence in Chicago, where he published the booklet *Apostolic Reunion in America*.

1910: *Declaration of Ecclesiastical Principles* made jointly with Msgr. Kaminski and Msgr. Miraglia-Gullotti. Pastoral letter on the subject issued 1 January. Vilatteville founded in Chihuahua, Mexico, on July 18: a farming settlement under the auspices of the SPB (Dismembered 10 May 1911 due to troubles caused by Mexican Revolution. Colonists transferred to New Mexico.) Former R.C. priest Enrico C. Carfora admitted to the Italian American Constituency and as successor to Rev. Lops in Youngstown, Ohio.

1911: Msgr. Kaminski entered into eternal rest on September 19. New church (St. Anne's) organized among Bohemian Americans at Montpelier (Kewaunee County), Wisconsin, on July 26.

1912: Italian American constituency incorporated as National Diocese in Ohio, on June 14. Reverend Carfora consecrated as diocesan bishop.

1913: On April 15, Hungarian American constituency organized in South Bend, Michigan. Rector Viktor de Kubyiny consecrated bishop and invested as knight commander of OCT. Bohemian church at Montpelier, Wisconsin, incorporated 22 September, with Rev. Lops as rector. He also ministered at Gardner and at Duval. On November 16, in New Jersey, Polish American Synod elected Josef Zielonka bishop. He was consecrated by Msgr. Miraglia-Gullotti.

1915: On June 20, Frederic Lloyd was ordained priest for Chicago and Samuel G. Lines for Los Angeles. American Catholic Church (ACC) Council incorporated in Illinois on July 13, 1915. In August Rev. Timothy V. Peshkoff ordained for a Byzantinen Rite constituency. November 6, Rev. Antonio Lenza received into the church with his parish of San Antonio de Padua, Hackensack, N.J.

On December 29, Rev. Lloyd consecrated as Bishop of Illinois. At that time, former Manitoba (Canada) R.C. missionary Casimir F. Durand ordained for St. David's Chicago and appointed as assistant (French ministry) at Our Lady Church. Also ordained: Rene Zawistowski for Polish ministry in Central Falls, Rhode Island.

1916:   On May 9, Msgr. Miraglia-Gullotti, half paralyzed came to live at Our Lady parish rectory in Chicago, with Msgr. Vilatte.

1917:   On October 24, birth of Rev. Durand's twin sons Rene and Paul, thus named after Msgr. Vilatte and Msgr. Miraglia-Gullotti. On December 16, board of trustees formed in Central Falls, Rhode Island (RI), for the purpose of building a Polish church. Members included Albert Ogara and Stanley Chmura.

1918:   Msgr. Miraglia-Gullotti entered into eternal rest in Chicago on July 25. Msgr. Carfora brought the Italian National Diocese under Old Roman Catholic bishop de Landas (whom he succeeded in 1919). Rev. Franciszek Kanski mitred. Rev. C.F. Durand missionary in Windsor, Ontario. Church centre located at 245 Ouellette Avenue. Also Principal of ACC Theological Department.

1919:   Established Our Lady of Nazareth Orphanage and Convalescent Home in Chicago. On May 18, dedicated

Rev. Zawistowski's church in Central Falls, Rhode Island.

1920: Presided synod in Chicago on April 10. Swedish American constituency formed under Bishop Carl Nybladh, consecrated on December 5.

1921: Ordained to the priesthood in Chicago, on September 27: George A. McGuire, M.D. and William Ernest Robertson for an African-American constituency (called African Orthodox Church /AOC). On September 28, Rev. Durand and Robertson assisted at and witnessed the consecration, by Msgr. Vilatte, of Dr. McGuire as Bishop Ordinary of the AOC. Bishop Nybladh was co-consecrator.

1922: Death of Father Jean Baptiste Gauthier in Green Bay (20 June). Wisconsin churches at Duval, Gardner and Green Bay turned into Anglican Rite parishes of the Diocese of Fond du Lac (Episcopal Chuch).

1923: In March admitted Bishop G..A. McGuire into OCT as Knight commander. Invested him in June at Good Shepherd Church (AOC), New York. Approved the founding of a parish church in Minneapolis, Minnesota, by Rev. C.F. Durand. In the month of June, having appointed Bishop Lloyd President of the ACC and put Father Durand in charge of the French-speaking Christian Catholics, he went into retirement to France. In October, at Gargan, he established Oeuvre Notre Dame de France: an extension of the Church in America. On October 10, he issued a bull allowing the consecration (on November 18) of Rev. W.E. Robertson as Coadjutor to Bishop G.A.

McGuire. On December 6, he appointed Rev. Maxime Adrot as Auxiliary in France.

1924:   On May 24 ordained Edmond Éthier at Gargan. Also ordained (in June): Charles-Alphonse Blanchette from Pittsburg. Asked to lead a National French Church by a group of politicians. On December 25, as a means of expressing filial sentiments, Msgr. Louis F. Giraud of France (Bishop Houssaye's successor), his auxiliary P.G.. Vigué and Austrian Regionary Bishop Alois Stumpfl named him Patriarch of the Gallican Episcopate. Rev. Axel Z. Fryxell of Seattle, Washington, was consecrated as Second Bishop of the Swedish American constituency on June 24.

1925:   Father Eugène Prévost of the *Fraternité Sacerdotale*, a religious order that takes care of aged clergy, made arrangements for Msgr. Vilatte to live with Cistercian Monks at Pont Colbert, near Versailles. He died there from a heart attack four years later, 1 July. Buried in Gonards' Cemetery 3 July.

Msgr. Vilatte's grave in Les Gonards Cemetery, Versailles, France

BIBLIOGRAPHY

PUBLISHED WORKS OF MSGR. VILATTE

ESSAYS

Apostolic Reunion in America, Chicago, 1909.

A Sketch of the Belief of the Old Catholics, Duval, 1890, in collaboration with Church Trustees Guillaume Barrette, Édouard Debecker and Augustin Marchand.

Autobiography. Written in 1910, under title A Pioneer Narrative. Posthumously published in 1933, by St. Willibrord Press, Chicago, with the title *A Personal Narration by the Most Reverend Rene Vilatte*. Re-edited in 1960, by H.G. de Wilmott Newman, with title *My Relations with the Protestant Episcopal Church*, Glastonbury, U.K.

Chivalrous and Religious Order of the Crown of Thorns Statutes, James Kerr & Sons, Forth Howard, Wisconsin, 11 August 1893, in collaboration with Reverend G.J. Fercken.

Declaration of Ecclesiastical Principles, Buffalo, January 1, 1910, in collaboration with Msgr. Paolo Miraglia-Gullotti and Msgr. Stefan Kaminski.

Ecclesiastical Relations between the Old Catholics of America and Foreign Churches, Duval, WI, 1892, in coll. with G. Barrette, E. Debecker & A. Marchand, A.

Encyclical to All Bishops Claiming to Be of the Apostolic

Succession, Duval, Wisconsin, November 1893.

Letter Concerning the Acceptance of the Protestant Episcopalian Faith by Bishop Kozlowski, Chicago, 1902.

Orphan and Convalescent Home of St. Mary of Nazareth, Chicago, 1919.

St. Peter in Rome?, Duval, Wisconsin, 1893.

The Society of the Precious Blood, in collaboration with J.B. Gauthier, Duval, 1888.

The Independent Catholic Movement in France, London, 1907.

The Most Reverend Vilatte (Gawas, ON) Papers (Scheme for promoting Immigration from France, etc.), 1902-1904, Library and Archives Canada, Ottawa, Microfilm C-7807, Vol. 258, File Part 1.

Vilatteville, Candelaria Station, Chihuahua: An Institution of the Society of the Precious Blood, Mexico, 1911.

CATECHETIC AND LITURGICAL MATERIAL

Catéchisme, Bryson ed., Philadelphia, 1886.
Livre de prière, Episcopal Publishing House, New York, 1886.

Mode of Receiving the Profession of the Old Catholic Faith from one Newly Converted, Chicago, 1919.

The Smaller Catechism, Duval, Wisconsin, 1893. 2nd edition, 1912.

The Smaller Missal, Green Bay, 1896.

REVIEWS

The Old Catholic (1891), **The Little Catholic Star** (1895), **The Catholic Truth** (1898), **The American Catholic** (1915

BOOKS, ARTICLES, TESTIMONIALS ABOUT MSGR. VILATTE OR HAVING RELATION TO HIM AND HIS WORK

Abramisov, David F., *Vilatte and Orthodoxy*, **The Orthodox World**, Vol. XII, No. 2, March-April 1969.

Archbishop Vilatte of Wisconsin, 6 column inches, in **The Chiniquy Collection**, Series 09, No. 103, A. Pequegnat, Elliot Lake, Ontario.

Ashmall, Donald H., **Statement of Tribute and Thanksgiving: Bishop Rene Vilatte, 1854-1929**, International Council of Community Churches, Frankfort IL, 2014.

Azevedo, Carmo, **Patriot and Saint. The Life Story of Bishop Mar Julius (Alvares)**, Panjim, 1988.

Bartoszek, Donald S., *Apostolic Succession of Joseph Rene Vilatte*, in **Old Catholics ... in the USA**, Archives of the Roman Catholic

Diocese of Green Bay, document No. 201, 1959-1960.

Byrne, Julie, **Remaking America's Largest Religion**
Columbia University Press, 2016.

Bricaud, Jean, **Notice sur le sacerdoce et l'épiscopat de Mgr Vilatte**, edited by Charcognac, Lyon, September 1927.

Chiniquy, Charles, *Pastor's Register,* in **The Chiniquy Collection**, Series 09, No. 001, A. Pequagnat, Elliot Lake, Ontario. Msgr. Vilatte is mentioned in the following sections: *Communicants received, 1881-1884, Ministers who graduated from our (Saviour's) College.*

Cogné, Daniel, *Les armoiries de J. René Vilatte, 1854-1929,* **L'Héraldique au Canada**, Vol. XIX, No. 3, September 1985.

Côté, Thomas G.A., *René Vilatte, missionnaire à Fall River, M.A.*, **L'Aurore**, Montreal, 1882.07.27; 1882.08.03; 1882.08.10; 1882.09.21.

French, S.J., article on Little Sturgeon (WI) Mission in **The Living Church**, 24 October 1885.

Gaworek, Leah, *Good Shepherd or Wolf in Sheep's Clothing: Joseph Rene Vilatte*, **Voyageur**, Green Bay WI, Winter/Spring 2004, p. 28-35.

Greene, Stanley, Testimony on Msgr. Vilatte's ministry in Wisconsin, Christian Catholic Church Collection, National Archives of Quebec (P103).

Greene, Stanley, *The Story of Sturgeon Bay's First Park*, **The Peninsula**, Sturgeon Bay, WI, Vol. 7, Summer 1963, p. 7.

Hamelin, Jean, **Le Père Eugène Prévost, 1860-1946**, Presses de l'Université Laval, Québec, 1999, p. 168, 331-332, 338.

Hogue, W.H., *The Episcopal Church and Archbishop Vilatte*, **Historical Magazine of the Protestant Episcopal Church**, XXXIV (1967), 36.

Klukowski, Constantine, **History of St. Mary of the Angels Catholic Church Green Bay WI**, Provincial (O.F.M.) Library, Pulaski WI, 1956. *Useful information found in Chapters VI & VII on St. Louis Church built by Msgr. Vilatte that served as first Polish R.C. Church of St. Mary of the Angels.*

Le Catholique Français, edited by Father Hyacinthe Loyson, Paris, Oct. 1890.

L'Étincelle, edited by Msgr. J.E. Houssaye, Paris, May & August 1902.

Marx, Joseph A., *Archbishop Vilatte and the Old Catholic Church of America*, Archives of the Roman Catholic Diocese of Green Bay, Wisconsin.

Parisot, Jean, **Mgr Vilatte, fondateur de l'Église vieille-catholique aux États-Unis d'Amérique**, Imprimerie Soudée, Tours et Mayence, 1899.

Registers of Baptisms, Marriages and Burials of Wisconsin churches of: Precious Blood, Gardner, St. Marie, Duval, and St. Anne, Montpelier, 1885-1922.

Samson, L.J.A. & Vilatte, René, *Institution Indépendante de Saint-Hyacinthe*, **Le Courrier de Saint-Hyacinthe** (Quebec), November 4, 1880.

The Catholic Truth, Buffalo, Vol. 1, No. 1, June 1898.

The Church Scholiast, September 1887, on Rev. Vilatte, model priest.

The Most Rev. Archbishop Vilatte, **The Independent Catholic**, Colombo, vol. 1. No 5, mai 1892.

Theriault, S.A., *Charles Chiniquy et les Églises catholiques-chrétiennes*, **Aujourd'hui Credo**, United Church of Canada, November 1999.

Thomas, Sunny, **Behold a Saint. The Life and Times of Parumala Mar Gregorios**, Printaid, New Delhi, 1977.

CHRISTIAN CATHOLIC CHURCH, COMMUNITY CHURCH MOVEMENT, FREE CHURCHES, ECUMENISM, GALLICANISM

American Catholic Quarterly Review, vol. 14 (1889).

Article in **Altkatholischer Volkskalendar**, Baden-Baden, 1898.

Boone, Ardis M., **Father Charles Chiniquy's Ledger**. Baptisms, Marriages, Burials: First St. Anne Catholic Church (1851), Christian Catholic Church (1858)...

Bretell, Caroline, **Following Father Chiniquy: Immigration, Religious Schism, and Social Changes in Nineteenth-Century Illinois**, Southern Illinois University Press, 2015.

Bristol, A.M., **Atlas of Kankakee Co., Illinois**, J.H. Baers & Co., Chicago, 1883, p.21.

Chiniquy, Charles, **Autobiographie**, Beauport Publisher, Saint Romuald, Quebec, 1986. Synthesis of his bestsellers *Fifty Years in the Church of Rome* and *Forty Years in the Church of Christ*.

Chiniquy, Charles, **Persécutions aux Illinois, de l'abbé Chiniquy, l'apôtre de la tempérance au Canada**, 1857. Microfilm, National Library of Canada, Ottawa, 1983.

Durand, Casimir F., **The Old Catholic Church and Other Writings**, Apocryphile Press, Berkeley, 2010.

Durand, Casimir F., *Libres, catholiques et gallicans*, posthumously published in **Le Gallican**, July 1997, p. 12.

Faith and Fellowship in the Community Church Movement: A Theological Perspective, Community Church Press, Homewood, 1986.

French, S.J., article on Mission of Bon Pasteur, Little Sturgeon, Wisconsin, **The Living Church**, 24 October 1884.

Harding, Bernard E. (Bro. William), **The Genesis of Old Catholicism in America**, Beati Pacifici, 1898.

Lloyd, Frederic E.J., **Smaller Catechism for the Use of American Catholics**, St. David's House, Chicago, 1915.

Lougheed, Richard, **The Controversial Conversion of Charles Chiniquy**, Clements Academic, Toronto, 2008.

Loyson, Hyacinthe, **Liturgie de l'Église gallicane**, suivie d'un abrégé du catéchisme et d'un programme de la réforme catholique, Grassart, Paris, 1891.

Meillon, Félix, **L'Ancien prêtre et le ministère évangélique**, Cahors, 1901.

Michaud, E., article in **Le Catholique national**, Berne, June 1897.

Natsoulas, Theodore, *Patriarch McGuire and the Spread of the African Orthodox Church to Africa*, **Journal of Religion in Africa**, Vol. XII, 2 (1981), p. 81-104.

Newhall, J.R., **Introducing the International Council of Community Churches**, Community Church Press, 1994, p. 4.

Parot, Joseph J., **Polish Catholics in Chicago, 1850-1920**, Northern Illinois University Press, 1981.

Perdriau, Henri, **Fiat Lux. La logique et le bon sens**, La Vérité, Woonsocket, Rhode Island, 1928

Roussin, Fr., **Catholiques non romains et catholiques romains**, 1906.

Shotwell, J.R., **In Christian Love. Deliberations on a Decade**, Community Church Press, Homewood, Illinois, 1991; **Manual for Ministry**, Community Church Press, 1986, and **Unity Without Uniformity**. History of the Community Church Movement, Community Church Press. 2nd edition in 1999.

Shute, Daniel, *An Inquiry into the Presbyterian Work of the French Canadian Evangelization: Critical Factors in its Foundation*, **Journal of the Historical Society of the Presbyterian Church of Canada**, 1981.

Terry-Thompson, Arthur C., **The History of the African Orthodox Church**, 1956.

Teyssot, Thierry, **Église gallicane. Histoire et actualité**, Bordeaux, 1994.

The Negro Churchman, New York, December 1923 and November 1924.

Thériault, S.A., *Charles Chiniquy, a man of conviction, passionate and fascinating, 1809-1899* (in French), **Credo**, United Church of Canada, November 1999, p. 3-8. *Charles Chiniquy and Christian Catholic Churches*, idem (in French), p. 9-10.

Thériault, S.A., *Jerome Pelletier from Sorel (Quebec) and family at the origin of the Christian Catholic Church in Wisconsin*, **French Canadian/Acadian Genealogists of Wisconsin Quarterly**, Vol. 20, No. 3, Winter 2005-2006, p. 90-93.

Thériault, S.A., *The Christian Catholic Church (ICCC): A Presentation* (in French), **Germaniques: Ahnengalerie**, Verlag/Ahnentafel, Quebec, Vol. 2, No.1, p. 4-11, January-April 2002.

Thériault, S.A., *The French-Canadian Community Church Movement*, **The Christian Community**, vol. 40, no 8, p. 1 & 4.

Thériault, S.A., *The French-speaking Catholic Reform Movement in America* (in French), **Credo**, op. cit., Vol. 30, No. 12 (Dec. 1983), p. 20-22.

Theriault, S.A., *Two Western Quebec Families at the origin of the Christian Catholic Church in Illinois and Wisconsin*, **French Canadian/Acadian Genealogists of Wisconsin Quarterly**, Vol. 19, No. 2, Winter 2004-2005, p. 48-59.

The Prayer Book According to the Christian Catholic Rite of Community Churches, Canadian Chapter of the I.C.C.C., Ottawa, 1992.

Trela, J., **History of the North American Old Roman Catholic Church**, Straz Printery, Scranton, 1979. Also *The Italian National Catholic Church*, **PNCC Studies**, vol. 2, 1981.

Wielewinski, Bernard, **Polish National Catholic Church, Independent Movements, Old Catholic Church and Related Items. An Annotated Bibliography**, East European Monographs, Boulder. Distributed by Columbia University Press, New York, 1990.

FREE CATHOLICISM, OLD CATHOLIC MOVEMENT

Dederen, Raoul, **Un réformateur catholique au 19e siècle: Eugène Michaud, 1839-1917**, Droz, Geneva, 1963.

Gauthier, Léon, **Le vieux-catholicisme**, Genève, 1952.

Michaud, Eugene, **La notion exacte de la réforme catholique**, Conférences sur la réforme catholique et la crise actuelle, Geneva, 1878.

Michaud, Eugene, **Programme de réforme de l'Église d'Occident**, Paris, 1872.

Thériault, S.A., *Bishop D.M. Varlet, from the Church of Quebec to the Utrecht Church Reform* (in French), **Revue d'histoire de l'Amérique française**, Montreal, Vol. 36, No. 2 (Sept.1982).

Thériault, S.A., **Bishop D.M. Varlet's New France Letters** (in French), Quebec University Press, 1986, 112 p.

Thériault, S.A., **Msgr. Dominique M. Varlet, Originator of the Old Catholic Episcopal Succession**, Apocryphile Press, Berkeley, 2010.

Theriault, S.A., *The Pastoral Approach of Bishop D.M. Varlet, 1678-1742* (in French), **Internationale Kirchlische Zeitschrift** (IKZ), Berne, July-September 1985, p. 180-188.

Thériault, S.A., *The Holy Trinity in Bishop Varlet's Theology at the Origin of Old Catholicism*" (in French), IKZ (Berne), October-December 1983, p. 234-245.

ANNEX

Articles of Incorporation of the Diocese

Whereas the Reverend Rene Vilatte, Bishop Elect of the Old Catholic Church of America, at Dyckesville[83] in said County of Kewaunee and State of Wisconsin, decerning it advisable to cause the (Cathedral Parish) of Ste Mary in said Dyckesville, County and State aforesaid, to be incorporated in the manner prescribed by Chapter 37 of the Laws of Wisconsin, entitled "An Act Supplementary & Amendatory of Chapter 91 of the Revised Statutes", entitled of "Religious Societies" approved March 8, 1883, for the purpose and powers by Statutes in such cases made and provided, and having complied with the provisions of incorporation by said Chapter 37, now therefore:

Know all by these present that we, Rene Vilatte, Bishop Elect aforesaid of the Old Catholic Church of America, aforesaid Reverend John B. Gauthier, Vicar (at Gardner), aforesaid Reverend Bernard E. Harding as Secretary, and William Barrette and Edward Debecker as laymen, hereby do associate ourselves for the purpose of incorporating said entity pursuant to Chapter 37 of the Laws of the State of Wisconsin, in such case made and provided, and the powers thereby prescribed.

The name of said (cathederal parish) hereby incorporated shall be St Mary's, and the location thereof shall be at Dyckesville in Kewaunee County, State of Wisconsin, and shall be connected with and under the control of said Old Catholic Church and under the supervision of the Old Catholic Bishop of the diocese in which said congregation is situated and his successors in office.

The purposes of this corporation are to purchase, accept, own and hold property, real and personal, for the use and benefit of such corporation, and to sell and dispose of the same for the same use and benefit, subject to the restrictions provided by the By Laws, and to do all things necessary for the proper transaction of the business and duties of said corporation, and to do and perform all things useful in the management of the temporal affairs of the Old Catholic Church of America and of said congregation, and for the benefit thereof, and of such members as may become attached and belong to said church, in conformity with such rules and regulations as may be established by its By Laws, and also to purchase, own, hold, regulate, control, manage or dispose of any Eleemosynary, Educational, Cemetery, Religious, or other property which it may acquire in connection with said Old Catholic Church and congregation thereof or which may be assigned to it by the Bishop or other person or persons.

The property, real and personal, which shall be purchased, accepted, owned or acquired by said congregation in connection with said Old Catholic Church and congregation, for the purposes of any Eleemosynary, Educational, Cemetery, Religious, or other property, shall be vested in said corporate name and shall be devoted solely for the purpose and object of this corporation and for the benefit thereof, and shall descend in perpetual succession to said corporation.

The Officers of said Corporation shall be a President, a Vice-President and a Secretary.

The said Reverend Rene Vilatte, Bishop Elect as aforesaid, his successor or administrator, or such other person as may be appointed according to the rules of the Old Catholic Church, or administrator for the time being, shall be Ex Officio President. The said Reverend John B. Gauthier Vicar as aforesaid or his successor shall be Ex Officio Vice-President. The Seretary shall be selected or chosen by the Board of Directors or a majority thereof, and the two laymen shall be chosen from the laymen of said congregation who are practising members as prescribed by the By Laws of this corporation.

The duties of the President, Vice-President and Secretary shall be such as are implied by their respective office and as may be prescribed by the By Laws of this corporation.

The Reverend Rene Vilatte Bishop Elect as aforesaid, and the said Reverend John B. Gauthier Vicar as aforesaid, shall be and remain members of this corporation as long as they shall be and remain respectively Bishop and Vicar as aforesaid, and the said Reverend B.E. Harding aforesaid shall be and remain a member thereof so long as he shall be and remain Secretary of said corporation and whenever either or all of them shall cease to be Bishop, Vicar or Secretary by reason of death, resignation, removed or otherwise. Then in that case their respective successor as Bishop, Vicar or Secretary shall be and become their respective successors as members or the corporation and in like manner they shall have perpetual succession.

The said Edward Debecker and William Barrette laymen as aforesaid shall be and remain members of this corporation for the tenure of two years from and after the 6th day of June 1888, and until their successors are chosen or selected as provided by the by laws of this corporation.

The Board of Directors may at any time, by a majority vote, remove any Secretary if they claim that the best interest of this corporation requires such removal.

This corporation is formed without capital stock and solely for the purpose herein before stated.

The election of the two laymen above named took place in Dyckesville on the 6th of June 1888, and shall therefore take place at on the 6th of June 1890, and triannually thereafter.

The said Directors by a majority vote may adopt such By Laws not contrary to the conditions and Laws of the State, the Statutes of the Diocese and the Discipline of the Old Catholic Church, as may be deemed necessary for the proposed government of this corporation and the management and business thereof, or the temporal affairs of such congregation which may become connected therewith or attached thereto.

Said By Laws may be altered or amended in the manner required and not otherwise. They should, before they take effect, be recorded by the Secretary in a book provided for that purpose and subscribed to by each of the Directors, or a majority thereof.

In witness whereof, we the said Incorporators have caused these articles of incorporation to be made out and signed by the President and Secretary in the presence of two witnesses at Dyckesville, Kewaunee County, State of Wisconsin, this 13th day of February 1890.

Signed and sealed in the presence of

William Barrette & Hubert Joachim

Rene Vilatte (seal)
Old Catholic Bishop Elect & President Ex Officio of this Corporation

Bernard E. Harding, Secretary (seal)

Be it known that on the 13th day of February 1890, personally appeared before me the above named Reverend Rene Vilatte as President, and the above named Reverend B.E. Harding as Secretary of the above named corporation, both known to be the persons or officers above mentioned and who have executed the above articles of incorporation to be the act and deed of said corporation for the uses and purposes therein mentioned.

Recorded March 25, 1890 at 8:00 A.M.

Joseph Wery, Notary Public Kewaunee County

Msgr. Vilatte (2nd) and Rev. J.B. Gauthier

Consecration Certificate bearing the Signatures of Consecrator Julius Alvares, US Consul William Morey and Church Official, Dr. Lisboa Pinto.

Articles of Incorporation of the ACC

We, the undersigned, J. René Vilatte, Frederic E.J. Lloyd and Louis R. Zawistowski, citizens of the United States, propose to form a corporation under an act of the General Assembly of the State of Illinois, entitled An Act Concerning Corporations, approved April 18, 1872.

The objects for which the corporation is formed are:

- to promote, foster, disseminate and maintain the religious principles and the profession of faith of the American Catholic Church (ACC), deriving its jurisdiction from the Holy See of Antioch;

- to establish and maintain a Primatial See and a religious organization throughout the Americas, with jurisdiction over all dioceses, parishes and members thereof belonging to and subscribing to the Faith and using the formalities of the Latin (Western) Rite of the ACC;

- to grant and vest authority and power in the Metropolitan Archbishop (or Primate) to acquire, purchase, have, receive, hold and convey property, real, personal and mixed of every kind and character and from whatever source or means acquired, derived, given, received, donated or conveyed for the uses and purposes and the maintenance of the dioceses and parishes within the jurisdiction of said Archdiocese and for the religious and charitable institutions under the jurisdiction and supervision of the Archbishop and his coadjutors and advisors;

- to establish churches, hospitals, infirmaries, schools, convents and monasteries, as well as all other religious, educational and charitable institutions for the preservation, treatment and cure of the afflicted, the teaching and practice of religious discipline, education and manual training of parishioners, adherents to the faith and converts;

- to unite and centralize, in a religious, social, educational and benevolent organization the members and their families belonging to the parishes, churches, societies and congregations within said jurisdiction and professing the religious principles of the faith of the ACC, as well as the persons considering that end;

- to consecrate bishops, ordain priests, deacons and monks, to receive men and women under religious vows, to consecrate churches, chancels and cemeteries; and to establish rules for the government of the same.

The management of the corporation and the jurisdiction of all matters pertaining to the objects, interests and power of the same, and the power to establish the rules for the government of the same, shall be vested in a Board of five Trustees, of which Board the Metropolitan Archbishop and his successors in office shall be ex-officio supreme Presiding Prelate and Supreme Official of said Board, all of whom are to be elected from and by the members adhering to the Faith in such manner and removed from office as the Board of Trustees shall by the the laws and rules of said Archdiocese direct.

The following persons are hereby selected as the Directors to control and manage said Corporation for the first year of its corporate existence: the Most Reverend Archbishop Joseph René Vilatte, Supreme Presiding Prelate and Supreme Official of said Board, Frederic E.J. Lloyd, Louis R. Zawistowski, George H. Nelson and Carl W. Miller, who shall be known and constitute all the members of the first Board of Trustees.

The Corporate Offices and Primatial See are located at the following address: 3657 Grand Boulevard, Chicago, County of Cook, Illinois, U.S.A.

NOTES

[1] He taught at Notre-Dame-du-Laus (1st schoolmaster), Saint-Hyacinthe and the Institut Français of Pointe-aux-Trembles, near Montreal, between 1874 and 1876

[2] Charles Chiniquy (1809-1899), a French-Canadian priest, was apostle of Temperance in Quebec and founder of the parish of St. Anne (Kankakee) in Illinois. He is at the origin of a reform from which came the Christian Catholic and Protestant congregations, Presbyterian and Baptist in particular. He was an exceptional preacher who raised the crowds.

[3] Msgr. Vilatte, Autobiography *A Pioneer Narrative*, Chicago, 1910.

[4] Under the Law on religious corporations of Québec, based on the statutes drafted by Msgr. Vilatte. The diocese, called *Ordinariat des vieux-catholiques d'Amérique*, has been, since 1983, the Christian Catholic Rite of the International Council of Community Churches.

[5] He was consecrated with the title of *Metropolitan Archbishop*.

[6] The ACC was organized on August 20, 1894, at a synod in Cleveland, Ohio. The Polish-speaking churches first joined, followed by other groups, starting with Italian-Americans.

[7] The Year Book of the Churches 1924, Federal Council of the Churches of Christ in America, New York, p. 13.

[8] The 1905 French law on the Separation of the Churches and State instituted the Associations for the exercise of religion (*associations cultuelles*).

[9] He was admired by his parishioners, says Stanley Greene (Interview on Msgr. Vilatte, University of Wisconsin at Green Bay), quoting the Rev. Parker Curtis (An Old Man's Love Story), who knew him in Wisconsin. All those who came in contact with Msgr. Vilatte testified of his kindness. "I visited him when he was parish priest at Duval, wrote Rev. Curtis, and he received us warmly ... I will never forget this scene: Maria Hay, a blind woman who was principal singer in the choir, put her arms around his neck and kissed him on the cheeks. It was a spontaneous expression of the deep affection she felt for her priest."

[10] Jointly with diocesan trustees Guillaume Barrette, Édouard Debecker and Augustin Marchand.

[11] The Old Catholic, vol. 1, no 1, 1892, and Le Réveil, Montreal, 1898.07.30

[12] The Old Catholic, vol. 8, no 1, Green Bay WI, 1898.

[13] *New Herzog Encyclopedia of Religious Knowledge*, 1911, p. 572-573.

[14] The Old Catholic, Advent 1893.

[15] A pastoral poem published in The Old Catholic, Lent 1895.

[16] The Little Catholic Star, October 1894.

[17] The Old Catholic, July 1895.

[18] The Old Catholic, 1911, New Schaff-Herzog Encycl. of Rel. Knowledge, 1911, p. 571.

[19] The Old Catholic, Vol. 4, No. 12, December 1895.

[20] R. Vilatte, *Chivalrous & Religious Order of the Crown of Thorns Statutes*, Fort Howard, Wisconsin, 1893, p. 7.

[21] The Detroiter Abenpost, 1894.01.03.

[22] Cleveland Plain Dealer, 1894.08.20 and *Polish American Studies*, Vol.40, No. 2, 1998.

[23] Rochester Democrat & Chronicle, 1894.09.30.

[24] March 1, 1902.

[25] December 19, 1915.

[26] Pawtucket R.I. newspaper, 1919.05.19.

[27] *The Republican*, Sturgeon Bay, 1891.05.14, and *Green Bay Daily Gazette*, 1892.08.25.

[28] Mentioned in *Histoire des Franco-Américains* by Robert Rumilly, Union Saint-Jean-Baptiste d'Amérique, 1958, page 153.

[29] St Joe Herald, January 1902.

[30] The Old Catholic, Vol. IV, No. 2, December 1895.

[31] Idem.

[32] Circular *Chivalrous Order of the Crown of Thorns*, Chicago, Oct. 1904.

[33] The Old Catholic, July 1895.

[34] *Scheme for promoting immigration to Canada (April 1, 1902)*, in **Msgr. Vilatte (Gawas, ON) Papers**, Library & Archives Canada, Microfilm No. C-7807, Vol. 258, Part I. And circular *Vilatteville, a farming community under the auspices of the Society of the Precious Blood in Chihuahua, Mexico*, July 1910.

[35] Circular *Orphan and Convalescent Home of St. Mary of Nazareth*, Chicago, 1919.

[36] L'Étincelle, No. 172, Paris, May 7, 1907.

[37] L'Étincelle, Paris, June 1907, p. 329-331.

[38] *Le Gallican*, February 1925.

[39] Biblical references are put in parentheses at the end of quotations, even where Msgr. Vilatte did not reference them.

[40] *Msgr. Casimir Durand, The Old Catholic Church and Other Writings*, Apocryphile Press, Berkeley, 2010, page 67.

[41] What was Catholic once…, pages 23-25.

[42] Defending Orthodox Catholic Truth, pages 17-19.

[43] Why we are not Romanist, pages 59-61.

[44] S.A. Thériault, *Msgr. Rene Vilatte,* op. cit.

[45] Defending Orthodox Catholic Truth, page 17, and What mean these stones?, page 47.

[46] We maintain the faith…, page 38.

[47] Why we are not Romanist, page 60.

[48] *Msgr. Rene Vilatte, Community Organizer of Religion*, page 104.

[49] Idem.

[50] We maintain the faith..., page 38.

[51] *Msgr. Rene Vilatte…,* op. cit., page 105.

[52] What was Catholic once…, pages 23-25.

[53] Since his election by the synod, at Duval (Kewaunee), Wisconsin, on November 16, 1889.

[54] By the separation of 1054, he means the rupture between the Church of Rome (West) and the Church of Constantinople (East). *Thereafter*, he

adds, *there have been many sects coming out of the Catholic Church to unite to Protestantism.*

[55] A pejorative term used to describe the doctrines of the Roman Church found to be outside the common Catholic path of undivided Christianity.

[56] Based on the profession of faith made at his episcopal consecration.

[57] This heresy, taught by the priest Arius (250-336), denied an essential point of the Christian faith: the divinity of Jesus Christ. It was condemned by the Council of Nicaea in 325.

[58] Nestorianism asserts that two persons, one divine, the other human, coexist in Jesus Christ. This thesis was defended by Nestorius, Patriarch of Constantinople (428-431).

[59] Monophysism affirms that Christ has only a divine nature. This goes against the dogma of the dual nature (human and divine) established by the Council of Chalcedon in 451.

[60] Wladimir Guettée, born René François Guettée (1816-1892), was a Roman Catholic priest who converted to orthodoxy. He has written many books on religious history which sparked controversy including *La Papauté hérétique* (Sandoz & Fishbacher, Paris, 1874).

[61] The full phrase reads: *Quod ubique, quod semper, quod ab omnibus creditum est.* It is attributed to Saint Vincent of Lerins and means: "that which was believed everywhere, always and by all". This is called the rule or criterion of catholicity of the Christian faith.

[62] The conversion of the substance of the Eucharistic elements into the body and blood of Christ at consecration.

[63] The early or apostolic age is traditionally the period of the twelve apostles, ranging from the Great Commission of the Apostles to the resurrected Christ until the death of the last apostle, regarded as that of the Apostle John in Anatolia around 100. https://en.wikipedia.org/wiki/Apostolic_Age

[64] Propitiation means: through the blood of His Son who expiated

them, God forgives our sins if we ask Him through Christ, our substitute and our advocate.

[65] This council, which is also called Synod of Jerusalem, was convened by Greek Orthodox Patriarch Dositheos Notaras in March, 1672. It reasserted traditional Orthodox doctrines about the Real Presence of Christ in the Eucharist and its decrees received universal acceptance as an expression of the faith of the Greek Orthodox Church.

[66] The Council of Trent was the 16th-century Council of the Roman Catholic Church. It is considered to be one of the Church's most important councils. It convened in Trent (then capital of the Bishopric of Trent, in the Holy Roman Empire, now in modern Italy) between December 13, 1545, and December 4, 1563. The Council defined Church teachings in the areas of Scripture and Tradition, Original Sin, Justification, Sacraments, the Eucharist and the veneration of saints. By specifying Catholic doctrine on salvation, the sacrament, and the Biblical canon, the Council was answering Protestant disputes.
http://en.wikipedia.org/wiki/Council_of_Trent

[67] The consecration certificate bearing the signature of Mr. William Morey (1837-1908), US Consul at Colombo, consecrator Julius Alvares and church official Lisboa Pinto is reproduced in the Annex, page 121.

[68] Reported in **Polish American Studies**, Vol. LV, No. 2, 1998.

[69] The priests and the faithful who founded independent parishes incurred excommunication. This has caused conflicts in Polish communities. The faithful Roman Catholics often saluted those of the independent parishes with the Polish word *Barabaszy* (traitors). The independent faction replied with the raillery *Rzymiany* (Romans). This screaming of names was often done in public. Even the funeral processions of the independents could be welcomed with the cry of *Barabaszy*.
http://clevelandmemory.org/ebooks/Polish/part03.html.

In this context of tension, the passions could be exacerbated to the point of causing exchanges of shots as we saw in Omaha (Nebraska) in 1895.

[70] Msgr. Vilatte was then bishop elect.

[71] 1,800 French Canadians and 300 Irish.

[72] Dedicated to Saint John The Baptist, patron of the French Canadians.

[73] A first meeting was held in May with the leaders: Moise Bessette, Eloi Jetté and Charles Leclaire, M.D.

[74] It was on Lot No. 6, Concession V, as indicated in the contract signed on June 11, 1898. It was a 105-acre lot located on the southeastern side of Desjardins Bay, later called Gawas Bay. It consisted of a house of seven rooms and an adjoining building, in which was the chapel.

[75] One of them was the Rev. Dr. Ernest C. Margrander. He was a theological advisor to Msgr. Vilatte. Part of his ministry was at the diocesan seminary in Chicago, where he taught church history and dogmatic theology. He wrote several articles in *The New Schaff-Herzog Encyclopedia of Religious Knowledge* (1912).

[76] He developed this topic in his booklet *St. Peter in Rome?*, Duval, 1893.

[77] The apostle does not speak of Rome in the figurative sense of Babylon, wrote Adam Clarke, but of the ancient city of Babylon in Iraq, which was the metropolis of the Jewish diaspora in the Middle East, in "Commentary on 1 Peter 5:13". **The Adam Clarke Commentary**, 1832.

[78] Alfonso Salmeron (1515-1585), author of studies on the New Testament. https://fr.wikipedia.org/wiki/Alfonso_Salmeron

[79] Such as its doctrinal infallibility and its jurisdiction over all the faithful, taken individually and collectively.

[80] The proposed colony was in Saskatchewan, near Rosthern, south of Basin Lake, in Townships 41 & 42, Ranges 23 & 24, W.2.M., and was called

Port Royal. Letter from J. Obed Smith, Commissioner of Immigration in Winnipeg, to Frank Pedley, Superintendent of Immigration in Ottawa (1902.08.21), **Msgr. Vilatte (Gawas ON) Papers,** Library and Archives Canada, Ottawa, Microfilm C-7807, Vol. 258.

[81] Apocryphal book included in the Vulgate of St. Jerome but excluded from the present Bibles.

[82] Saint Gregorios of Parumala (1848-1902) was a bishop of the Malankara Orthodox Church of India. He became a priest at the age of 18, a bishop at the young age of 28. He died at the age of 54 and was buried at SS Peter and Paul Church, Parumala. In 1947, he was declared as a saint. He is the first canonized Christian saint from India.
https://en.wikipedia.org/wiki/Geevarghese_Mar_Gregorios_of_Parumala

[83] The location identified as *Dyckesville* (Kewaunee County) in the Articles of Incorporation of 1888, was later named *Duvall*, from the settlement that emerged in the vicinity of St. Mary's church. It is not the currently named Dyckesville, a place located partially in the town of Red River, Kewaunee County and partially in the town of Green Bay, Brown County. Dykesville, the first placename, was from the nearest settlement at the time the mission was established.

www.ingramcontent.com/pod-product-compliance
Lightning Source LLC
Chambersburg PA
CBHW031137090426
42738CB00008B/1125